THE ULTIMATE
PRIVACY
FIELD
GUIDE

THE ULTIMATE

PRIVACY FIELD GUIDE

A WORKBOOK OF BEST PRACTICES

EDITED BY ERIN BERMAN AND BONNIE TIJERINA

ALA OFFICE FOR INTELLECTUAL FREEDOM (OIF)

ALA
Editions

CHICAGO 2023

ERIN BERMAN is a fierce privacy advocate who led the Privacy Subcommittee of ALA's Office for Intellectual Freedom from 2018 to 2022. During her time as innovations manager for the San José Public Library, she published the book *Your Technology Outreach Adventure: Tools for Human-Centered Problem Solving*. Currently, she works as the division director of the Learning Group for the Alameda County Library in California.

BONNIE TIJERINA is a researcher, librarian, and community convener. She is currently focused on creating opportunities for education and discussion in the library profession and beyond on the role libraries and librarians can play in the increasingly complex issues of the digital world. In that space, she has worked on several grant-funded projects that involve privacy and big data research ethics, and she is the coeditor of *Protecting Patron Privacy: A LITA Guide*. She is also the founder and annual coordinator of the Electronic Resources & Libraries Conference.

This project was made possible in part by the Institute of Museum and Library Services LG-36-19-0073-19.

Extensive effort has gone into ensuring the reliability of the information in this book; however, the publisher makes no warranty, express or implied, with respect to the material contained herein.

ISBN: 978-0-8389-3730-3 (paper)

Library of Congress Cataloging-in-Publication Data

Names: Berman, Erin, editor. | Tijerina, Bonnie, editor.
Title: The ultimate privacy field guide : a workbook of best practices / edited by Erin Berman and Bonnie Tijerina, Office for Intellectual Freedom.
Description: Chicago : American Library Association—ALA Editions, [2023] | Includes bibliographical references and index. | Summary: "Designed for use in school, public, and academic settings of all shapes and sizes, this easy-to-use workbook is packed with practical, hands-on exercises to guide you towards creating a more privacy-focused library"—Provided by publisher.
Identifiers: LCCN 2022029484 | ISBN 9780838937303 (paperback)
Subjects: LCSH: Privacy, Right of. | Intellectual freedom.
Classification: LCC JC596 .U57 2023 | DDC 323.44/8—dc23/eng/20220729
LC record available at https://lccn.loc.gov/2022029484

Original design by Heejung Yoon, Ryan Carnrick at PixelbyInch.com.
Layout adapted by Kim Hudgins.

♾ This paper meets the requirements of ANSI/NISO Z39.48-1992 (Permanence of Paper).

Printed in the United States of America
27 26 25 24 23   5 4 3 2 1

CONTENTS

ACKNOWLEDGMENTS

We would especially like to thank the academic, public, and school libraries that were willing to be test libraries. Your feedback from real-world experiences with the guides has been invaluable in making these useful for many more libraries.

Thanks to those who helped us write guides, including Becky Yoose and Emily Ray, and those who reviewed the guides, made up mostly of members of ALA's Privacy Subcommittee. Thanks to Julie Oborny, our UX specialist who helped us better understand the users of the guides.

Big thanks to Deborah Caldwell-Stone and everyone in ALA's Office for Intellectual Freedom for their advice and support throughout the grant.

INTRODUCTION

With the creation of ever larger datasets and methods to track users' every movement online, library workers need to have a deep understanding of privacy, confidentiality, and security. While privacy is a core value of librarianship, it often feels like an overwhelming and onerous undertaking. Library workers need easy-to-use tools that will help them create private and secure spaces for users to express their intellectual freedom.

The editors of this book, Bonnie Tijerina and Erin Berman, saw that there was a lack of practical how-to guides for making concrete privacy changes in the library. As a librarian and researcher, Bonnie has focused on the role libraries play in supporting their communities in the digital space. As an active member and then chair of the Privacy Subcommittee of ALA's Office for Intellectual Freedom, Erin has heard often from library workers who feel passionately about supporting users' privacy rights but feel unprepared, not tech-savvy enough, or not in the right position of leadership to make a change.

To address the concerns voiced by library workers, Bonnie and Erin partnered to create the "Privacy Field Guides." Sponsored by the Institute of Museum and Library Services and the American Library Association, these short online guides are designed to work in school, public, and academic libraries, making it easier to talk about privacy and take steps, even small steps, to improve the library's or its users' privacy in some way.

This publication gathers those guides together into one workbook, with each chapter representing a guide that covers topics important to library workers, including the basics of digital security, understanding the data lifecycle, performing library privacy audits, and writing or reading privacy policies. The chapters also help libraries learn how to talk about privacy with stakeholders, how to work with vendors to secure privacy requirements, and what to consider around nontechnical privacy issues.

This workbook has been thoroughly reviewed and then vetted in real-world library settings. Library stakeholders from across the country participated in surveys, trainings, workshops, and focus groups to provide input and guidance about the content and format of these guides. Library privacy experts wrote the guides, which were then put through real-world testing before reaching their final versions.

The workbook chapters are structured to give library workers the tools they need to create and be advocates for a safer, more secure library. Each chapter will give an introduction to the topic and then provide several exercises for you to implement privacy changes at your library. Each chapter follows the same easy-to-use format. You can read this workbook cover to cover, but we imagine you will choose a chapter that interests you or is in an area that your library would like to work on. Then you can revisit this workbook several times to learn about other aspects of privacy.

While some of the work in these chapters may not seem like big steps, these small but consistent actions can have large implications for your community. Learning the language to advocate for privacy, tweaking physical spaces, using new digital security tools, rethinking policies and practices, and asking questions within your organization will make a difference. With many libraries taking these steps, there is the possibility for powerful, collective change.

Digital Security Basics

Understanding basic digital security concepts, and knowing where to go for more help, is a great first step for all who work in libraries. Not only will these skills help make the library and its data more secure, but they will also allow staff to better help users to be more secure online. This chapter is intended for individuals who want to learn digital security skills and for those hoping to provide privacy and digital security education for library staff.

In This Chapter

1

Creating Strong, Secure Passwords

Do you lock your house when you leave for the day? Most of us probably would answer "yes" to this question. Why do we secure the door? We lock our homes because we have things inside that we don't want anyone else to have access to or steal. Creating a strong password is like having a unique key and lock to your house. We have to make sure that those locks are strong!

Passwords Are Out, Passphrases Are In

Remembering passwords for eighty different accounts is a challenge. We want to have a unique password for every account, and this can get out of control quickly. How can a person be expected to come up with a secure password that can also be remembered? Passphrases!

EXERCISE

Practice making a passphrase. The strongest passphrases will have at least seventeen characters (and spaces count).

1. Think of a set of words that have meaning to you and that you'll remember. Do not include any personal information such as birthdates, addresses, or names. String together a combination of these words to create a random phrase.

2. Add numbers and symbols to the phrase at the beginning, middle, or end.

3. Now, test your passphrase (https://howsecureismypassword.net) and see how quickly it can be broken.

QUICK TIP
Forget about replacing "i" with "1" or "for" with "4." These techniques are so common now that the computer programs that crack passwords know them too.

Password Managers

TRY A PASSWORD MANAGER
Dashlane:
dashlane.com
1password:
1password.com
LastPass:
lastpass.com

How many passwords are you expected to remember at work? Do you have them written down on a sticky note that's placed "discreetly" under your keyboard or in an office drawer? Believe it or not, one of the most common ways hackers gain access to accounts is through the person responsible for keeping their accounts safe. One solution to too many passwords is using a password manager.

Password managers generate and store complex passwords for you. You just have to remember one (very secure and unique) master password for the manager itself, and everything else is taken care of for you. Also, organizations can utilize a team password manager to manage shared accounts.

- Explore the password manager suggestions in this chapter. Then set up an account and try it out for a week.

- Use your strongest passphrase as the password for your password manager.

Multi-Factor Authentication

QUICK TIP
Are you saving your passwords with your browser? Watch out. This is not secure and is easily hacked. Password managers make it much harder for anyone to access your complex passwords and phrases.

For accounts that hold a lot of our personal information, we want to make sure we're the only ones with access. *Multi-factor authentication* (MFA) means that just entering a password on the computer isn't enough for someone to gain access to your account. The term *2-factor authentication* is commonly used as well, and is a subset of MFA that only requires one additional factor in addition to your password to grant access.

With MFA, when you enter a password into a digital account, you will be prompted to verify your identity through another means. Most often you will be texted a code to the phone number on file. That code would then need to be entered into the account to gain access. Sometimes MFA will utilize an authorization app, use a physical object like a security token, or request a biometric identifier.

If you ever see one of these texts come to you when you're not trying to access the account, then you know someone else is attempting to break in. This is a good time to change your password.

EXERCISE

- Review your personal accounts and enable MFA where possible. In the table below, list the current accounts you have, whether or not they have multi-factor authentication, and if they do, what that verification involves.

ACCOUNT	MULTI-FACTOR AUTHENTICATION (Y/N)
Email	Y - password, text code, second email verification, phone call

- Multi-factor authentication can also be used at the library. Can you think of any accounts that could benefit from adding multi-factor authentication?

Phishing

Phishing is the practice of sending fraudulent e-mails that claim to be from reputable sources to trick users into revealing personal information that can then be used for illicit or malicious purposes. Most libraries have filtering software for their e-mail accounts, but this doesn't mean you shouldn't be on the lookout for phishing e-mails.

Avoid Getting Caught

QUICK TIP

If you have clicked on a link you think might be malicious, let your IT staff know right away.

- Only click links in e-mail from trusted sources.

- Don't download an attachment unless you know who it's from.

- Don't enter your personal information into any form you have reason not to trust.

- Use context clues and listen to your gut. Just because an e-mail looks like it's from a coworker doesn't guarantee that it is. A hacker can send a message that appears to be from your coworker by hacking or spoofing their e-mail address.

- Look at the entire URL you are being asked to click on. Is it exactly the same as the site address you normally type?

Example of a Phishing Scam

Rachael Prestrio <president973@aol.com>
Today, 9:55 AM

Kelly, Are you free at the moment?

Regards
Rachael Prestrio | Libary Staff

Wilson, Kelly
Today, 2:09 PM

Do you still want to talk?
Sorry, I was in meeting.

Kelly Wilson | Manager, Twin Peaks Public Library

Rachael Prestrio <president973@aol.com>
Today, 2:15 AM

Yeah i just need you to do something for me. I am tied up right now, can you purchase Itunes gift card 3 pieces - $100 each? I would reimburse you when am through. If you go to this site you can purchase the girft cards https://itunes.gcardbonza.ltd/?=53gs4. let me know!

Regards
Rachael Prestrio | Libary Staff

Q: What are the phishing red flags in this e-mail between employees at different libraries?

A:
- The e-mail domain is from AOL. This is not a typical domain used by libraries.
- The response e-mail asked for money.
- There are several typos.
- The recipient is asked to visit a link and provide personal information.

Malware = Malicious Software

Malicious software is software designed to do damage or other unwanted actions to your computer or smartphone. Usually this type of software is installed on your computer when you download attachments in e-mails or click on unknown links or ads. It can also be installed when someone puts an external flash drive into your machine. If you open an e-mail and don't know what the attachment is, don't download it!

Activities to Secure the Library Workplace

- Check if your computers have antivirus software installed on them. Do the computers for users have the same protections as staff computers?

- Check to see if your mobile devices are updated to the latest version of the operating system (OS) they use.

- Create a schedule to regularly update the OS and software when updates are released, as malware can exploit security holes. You should check computers and all mobile devices.

- Does your library allow the use of external flash drives? Create procedures that do not allow staff to put external flash drives from users into staff terminals.

Ransomware

One type of malware gaining in popularity is ransomware. How does it work?

Attackers gain access to your computer when you accidentally download malware, and then they hold your information hostage. The attackers may lock all your files or shut down your entire network, and they will require you to pay them to regain access. If files are important to you, make sure to back them up to external drives or a cloud server.

These attacks often focus on businesses and governments so watch out for suspicious e-mails at work. If it feels wrong, report it to your IT department. If you see a suspicious e-mail in your personal account, mark it as spam (if possible) and delete the e-mail without clicking on anything.

QUICK TIP
Check to see if your work or personal e-mail has been compromised by going to https://haveibeen pwned.com.

QUICK TIP
Regularly update your devices. Updates are often security patches. Your apps and software are only protected when you're running the latest version of them.

EXERCISE

1. Perform a search for news reports of ransomware attacks on libraries. How many libraries can you find that have experienced attacks?

_____

_____

_____

2. Does your library have a plan in place for a ransomware attack? Connect with your IT department and ask them the questions below. If no plan exists, try to develop one.

   - How will staff be contacted without access to e-mail?

   - How will users be notified of a ransomware attack?

   - Does the library have a method for users to check out materials without access to the ILS?

Network Privacy

Pull up your library website. Look in the address bar. Do you see a little lock that's closed or open? Does your web address say HTTP or HTTPS? The "S" at the end of HTTPS stands for "Secure." It means that all communications between your browser and the website are encrypted, so no one else can see the data that is being sent.

It is very important that your library website use HTTPS (rather than just HTTP), especially on the accounts page. People visiting your site without HTTPS may even get warnings from their browsers telling them your site is not secure.

Getting Your Website to HTTPS

How can you move your library's website from HTTP to the HTTPS protocol? First, connect with your IT manager, or get ready to start the process yourself if you're the one with network access. Seek out the options for purchasing certificates for either SSL or TLS—the two standard security technologies that are used in HTTPS. If costs are a concern, check out Let's Encrypt (https://letsencrypt.org). Let's Encrypt offers free certificates to anyone who owns a domain name. There is a robust community of support available to help install the certificates and get your site secured.

EXERCISE

1. Go to your library's website. Is it secured with HTTPS?

2. If your site is still operating with HTTP, connect with the IT department or get ready to start the process if you're the one with network access. Seek out options for purchasing SSL/TLS certifications.

3. If your site is secured, visit a few library vendors to see if their sites are secure.

Staff and User Training

Once you understand the basics, it's time to share that knowledge in your library. When thinking about staff training, consider the following:

- How to get staff buy-in. Explain to your staff why privacy is important and vital to library operations.

- How to upgrade the technical skills of your staff with regard to digital security and privacy. Start out with the basics. This chapter is meant to support all staff members, including those who are less tech-savvy.

- Consider ways to measure improvements after training and ways to keep the conversation going.

Even a short staff development session with the topics above will make the library, the staff, and your users safer. Use the lessons and activities from this chapter to host a staff or user training session. You can also use library privacy and security training materials that are available online. You can find all of the following resources at www.ala.org/advocacy/privacy/training:

- Staff training resources from NYC Digital Safety: Privacy and Security, the Data Privacy Project, and the Library Freedom Institute

- Programming for students at academic libraries

- User programming for public libraries

- Lesson plans for students at K–12 libraries

Digital Security Detective

You've now learned the basics of digital security. Practice your new skills by reading the following two accounts of library workers in the field.

Meet Jamie

Jamie works in technical services at a nearby community college library and also does a few hours at the reference desk. Jamie comes to work and logs into her computer, the ILS, a messaging app to communicate with colleagues, and the intranet. She was using one password for all these accounts but was told to create complex, unique passwords for each account by the IT staff. It was too hard to remember them all, so she keeps a handwritten list in her desk drawer.

When she's working at the reference desk, Jamie has to log into everything again and remember to log out at the end of her shift because she's using a shared computer. Sometimes she brings her list with all the passwords out to the reference desk where she keeps it in an unlocked drawer. At the end of every shift she brings it back to her desk, except for a couple of times when she's forgotten and picked it up the next morning. What recommendations would you make to improve her digital security practices?

Meet Mel

Mel works as an adult librarian at a busy public library. Yesterday, a user came to the service desk explaining that he was having trouble with the computer. He told them that he wanted to print a very important document, but was not able to do this from the public terminal. Mel started walking the user back to the public terminals only to discover that all of them were being used. Mel felt a moment of panic. The user told Mel that he was late to a job interview and needed to bring this document with him or he wouldn't be hired. He told Mel that he had a USB drive and asked them if they could print the document using a staff computer.

Mel, wanting to help the user get that job, agreed. Mel took the USB drive to their desk in the back, opened the document, printed it, and returned the USB drive to the user. The user seemed overwhelmingly thankful and left the library in a hurry. When Mel came into work the next day, all of the computers were offline and IT staff were running around frantically. Mel found a manager who explained that the library had been hit with a ransomware attack. All of the computers across the entire system were locked and the perpetrators were demanding a large payment of Bitcoin to return access to the library. What digital security mistakes were made by Mel in this scenario?

_____

_____

_____

_____

_____

_____

CHAPTER 2

How to Talk about Privacy

If you are reading this chapter, you know privacy is an important topic for libraries, and you also know that others might not necessarily share the same history, professional principles, understanding, or interest in the topic as you do. Finding ways to communicate the importance of privacy and why libraries should care about it is a critical way to make needed changes that can lead to safer environments for library users, library staff, and our communities. This chapter is meant to help you consider the best way to communicate about privacy—by thinking about the people you are trying to reach. It will also provide you with suggestions on the best messaging to use with various constituencies and stakeholders.

In This Chapter

Who Are You Trying to Reach?

When speaking about privacy concerns, you need to understand the motivations and interests of the group or individual you are communicating with. Possessing this understanding will make the conversation easier and more successful. Knowing your audience will help you talk about privacy in a way that is meaningful for them, not just for you. You can adjust your talking points and tactics once you understand who you're talking to, what they may already know, and what they care about.

One quick way to understand who you're talking to is by using an empathy map. An empathy map is a tool to better understand where someone or a group is coming from and how they see a particular issue, like privacy. While empathy maps are often derived from interviews with an individual, you may be able to learn more by filling in what you know and what you can learn about a person or group.

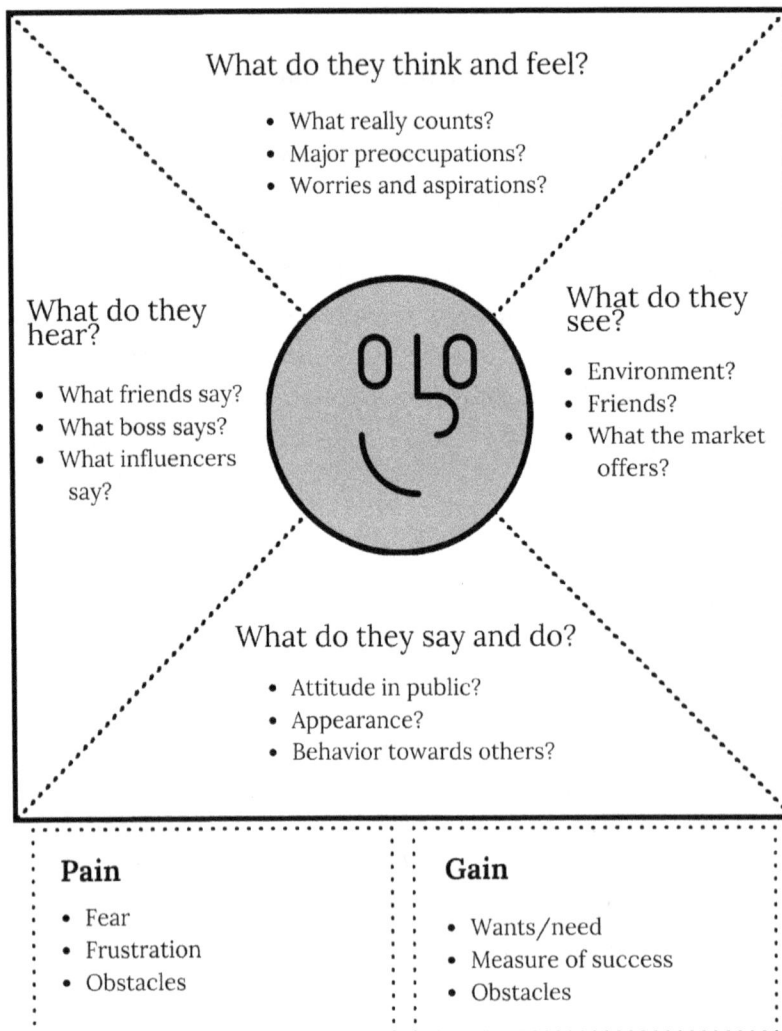

What do they think and feel?

- What really counts?
- Major preoccupations?
- Worries and aspirations?

What do they hear?

- What friends say?
- What boss says?
- What influencers say?

What do they see?

- Environment?
- Friends?
- What the market offers?

What do they say and do?

- Attitude in public?
- Appearance?
- Behavior towards others?

Pain

- Fear
- Frustration
- Obstacles

Gain

- Wants/need
- Measure of success
- Obstacles

This is a sample empathy map. Use it to help you better understand the motivations of those you're trying to reach

EXERCISE

Think of a stakeholder (an individual, group, community member, trustee, etc.) you need to talk to about a privacy-related concern. Fill out an empathy map. Think about what might motivate the stakeholder, what they might already know, and why they would care about privacy.

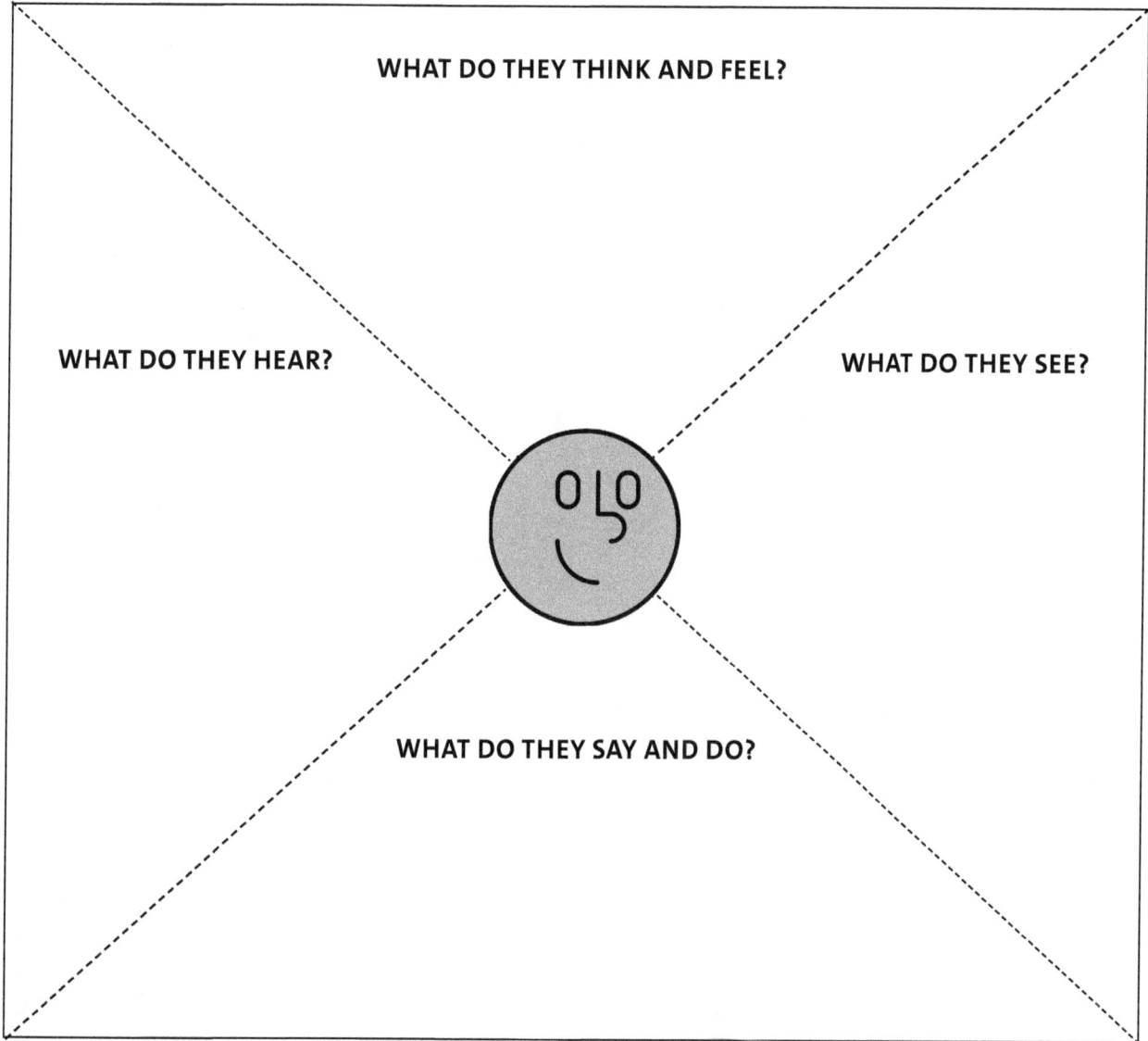

WHAT DO THEY THINK AND FEEL?

WHAT DO THEY HEAR?

WHAT DO THEY SEE?

WHAT DO THEY SAY AND DO?

PAIN

GAIN

EXERCISE

Once you fill out your empathy map, answer the following questions:

1. Who are you trying to talk to?

   _____

   _____

2. What motivates them regarding privacy?

   _____

   _____

3. What message could create a hook to interest them or to influence their view of privacy?

   _____

   _____

   _____

General Talking Points

Now that you have a good idea of who you'll be talking to, you can consider some high-level messages and conversation starters. It's helpful to have some talking points that have already been gathered by and for the library community. Consider the points listed below as you think about the empathy map exercise you just did.

- Privacy is essential to the exercise of free speech, free thought, and free association.

- Privacy is a human right.

- Lack of privacy and confidentiality discourages individuals' choices about what they read or view, thereby suppressing access to ideas and how they learn in the world.

- Libraries are a cornerstone of democracy and help ensure that Americans are able to read, research, and think freely.

- The possibility of surveillance, whether direct or through access to records of speech, research, and exploration, undermines a democratic society.

- Systems reflect the biases of their creators and can bias the ways that data is collected and used.

- The library community recognizes that children and youth have the same rights to privacy as adults.

- Most states have statutes declaring library records as confidential documents. The two remaining states, Hawaii and Kentucky, have had opinions issued by their attorneys general finding library records to be confidential documents.

- Librarians have a responsibility to protect the privacy of their users while responding to national security concerns within the framework of the law.

- Privacy is an equity issue—individuals should have the ability to give their consent to be surveilled or not. This type of permission should not be held by only the privileged few.

EXERCISE

Would these talking points be effective with the group or person you are trying to talk with? Which ones might resonate or not? Why? Alternatively, think about your audience. What other talking points can you think of that might resonate more with your audience? Write your thoughts below.

Getting Your Privacy Point Across

An elevator speech is a short description that communicates a concept or idea in such a way that the listener can understand it in a short period of time.

Sometimes we only have a few minutes (or less) to generate enough interest for the conversation to continue. Creating a succinct elevator speech can go a long way to getting and keeping someone's attention while quickly summarizing the idea or argument you're trying to convey. Your elevator speech should be interesting and concise. Ideally, it should also be memorable, so that your message is not forgotten. Here's a quick way to create an elevator speech:

1. Determine your goal. What is the end goal of this brief conversation?

2. Consider including a talking point (like those listed in the previous section) that will grab the listener's attention.

3. Summarize your argument or the point you're trying to make in as short a way as possible.

4. End with what you believe to be the solution and possibly how you can help the listener get there.

5. You may also want to include a "next step" so there's a clear next action.

Example

Let's say you're looking to appear before a board or campus assessment committee that is making a decision on a new analytics tool. You have just a few minutes with one of the members of the board or committee. Your goal is to convince this person that you have privacy concerns and would like to address the larger group to further the discussion on this product. You might say, "I know you and the board are deciding on product X for the library. There are some privacy concerns for our users with that product. Did you know research shows that being tracked makes people self-censor? Libraries are one of the few places left where we allow freedom of thought, uncensored. In fact, it's part of the ALA's Library Bill of Rights that we advocate for, educate about, and protect people's privacy, safeguarding all library use data, including personally identifiable information. I know this is a complex issue, and I would love to present this perspective to the board/committee for consideration."

EXERCISE

Use the talking points provided above, or create your own, to write an elevator speech in the space below for your targeted group or individual.

_____

_____

_____

_____

_____

Creating Persuasive Arguments

"I don't have anything to hide."

"Privacy is dead."

"I care about my privacy, but it's too late to do anything about it."

"Why do libraries care about my privacy?"

"We don't have the budget for privacy initiatives."

These are just a few of the reactions you might get when you start to engage library users, library staff, administration, stakeholders, or even your neighbors on topics related to privacy. Awareness of the value of privacy has become more mainstream as we hear about data breaches and tech companies' use of our data. But awareness does not necessarily mean understanding or comprehension of the true scope of the threats to our privacy; indeed, users may not yet understand that there are a myriad of small things we can do to protect our own or our community's privacy.

If your elevator speech led to further conversation or you are jumping right into talking about privacy with a group or individual, being able to make a persuasive argument is key. Consider strategies that could be used based on who you are addressing and what you learned about them in your empathy map.

- Be well-informed. Do the research to argue your point(s) so you can provide facts to back up your claims and concerns.
- Be specific. What are you looking for your audience to do?
- Be authentic. Explain why you care about this issue.
- Use metaphors.
- Find commonalities.
- Tell a story. Storytelling can help people visualize the impacts of their decision.
- Use repetition to remind people of your point or argument.

Library Privacy Advocacy

Maybe talking with others about privacy concerns has left you feeling that you would like to do more at your library, or even take part in a broader set of advocacy work on privacy-related issues. Below are ways to be a library privacy advocate:

- Talk about privacy. This goes a long way toward normalizing privacy as something to think about and discuss.
- Say something when you see something.
- Push back against non-privacy conventions.
- Build and use the collective voice. Find like-minded people or organizations where you can find others in support of privacy values.
- Educate and teach others. This could even be sharing an article with coworkers.
- Point people to the advocacy work that is already being done.

Are you looking for a way to work with others who are advocates in the library field? Here are a few organizations to check out: ALA's Privacy Subcommittee, the Library Freedom Project, ALA's Office for Intellectual Freedom, the Electronic Frontier Foundation, and the Digital Library Federation's Working Group on Privacy and Ethics in Technology.

EXERCISE

Imagine you get pushback during your privacy conversations. Build a persuasive argument to refute this.

Case Studies

Below are examples of scenarios that could use library privacy advocates. These scenarios are based on real-life examples and represent public, academic, and school libraries.

1. At a public library, the library foundation wants access to user data in ILS records. They want to send mailers to all library users, and so they have asked library staff to provide them with all the PII (personally identifiable information) from the library's ILS.

2. A caregiver or teacher asks a library worker about gaining access to a child's library use records. The caregiver explains that their child is a minor and so therefore they should be allowed to see the child's records. Or, the teacher is seeing a child fall behind and wants to make sure the child is using the library to do the work they say they are doing.

3. A university wants the library to use proctoring software that uses facial recognition for testing students. At the same time, the American Library Association passed a resolution opposing the use of facial recognition software in libraries. How do you persuade the university's governing bodies to not use this software?

4. The library board is over the moon about a particular vendor. They love the vendor's latest products and know many users would use it. The vendor does not meet the library's privacy requirements, but the board insists that "no one cares about privacy."

EXERCISE

Pick a scenario from one of the four given. Use this chapter to figure out how you would talk about, and advocate for, privacy in one of these scenarios.

Talking about Privacy

It must be noted that organizational culture will play a big role in your ability to have privacy discussions. Where you are within your organization and its culture will greatly impact your ability to start or continue privacy conversations. If the culture does not allow for front-line staff or lower management to have much say in operational matters, there may be other ways to exert influence. Perhaps you can identify and engage with potential allies who have more status in the organization and share similar perspectives with you.

While this chapter has mostly focused on how to start conversations about privacy, remember that continuing the conversation and building relationships is important, especially if you're hoping for long-term and sustainable privacy practices. You're looking for commonalities and ways to build relationships that will keep these conversations going into the future. Finding ways to communicate the importance of privacy and why libraries should care is a critical way to make needed changes that will lead to safer environments for library users, library staff, and our communities.

CHAPTER 3

Non-Tech Privacy

P rivacy is a fundamental right of library users. When most people think of privacy, they think of technology. However, threats to our privacy can come from both hi-tech and low- or no-tech practices. This chapter is meant to help you navigate some areas in your library that are often overlooked when thinking about privacy. You don't have to be a tech whiz or have access to your library's catalog, vendors, or information technology to enact healthy privacy practices. Use this chapter to help your library protect users' privacy, even when they're not online.

In This Chapter

Creating Private Spaces

The design of a library space can hinder or enhance privacy. Most staff are locked into the physical space they have, but a lot can be done with furniture to make the library inviting while also giving the maximum amount of privacy to your users. Everyone should have spaces where they can look at information without a passerby seeing what they're reading or typing.

Many users depend on the library for access to a computer. From students in school to the public in library branches, our users deserve privacy when using a computer. Adults may be filling out sensitive documents that contain their Social Security or credit card numbers. Children may be seeking out information on personal health or gender identity. College students may be exploring deep research on topics that might seem dangerous or offensive to the casual passerby. It doesn't matter why a user accesses a library computer; we are responsible for upholding that user's right to privacy.

Creating private spaces can feel tricky when libraries also need to consider the safety of their users. Library workers often want to be able to see all corners of the library, especially where children and teens hang out. However, situating furniture so that staff can surveil users denies them the right to privacy. Simple furniture moves can often allow for both privacy and safety.

QUICK TIP

If your library has the financial means, purchase privacy screens for all public computer terminals and provide laptops for more private browsing. Having headphones available for use or purchase is another way to provide a more private experience for users.

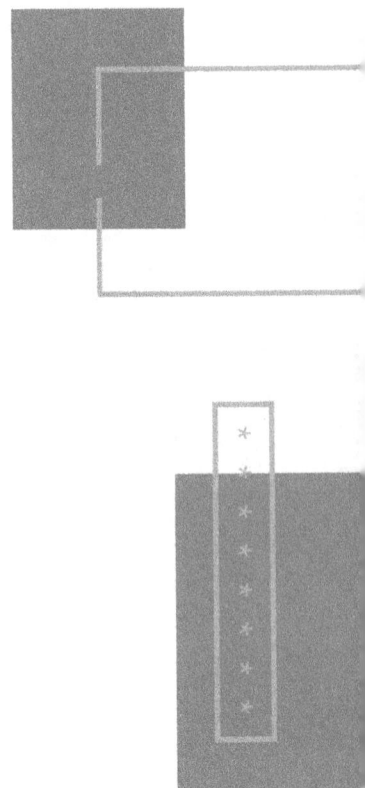

EXERCISE

Walk Around Your Library

Take a walk around your library. Can you identify any spaces where there are opportunities to create more privacy? Consider setting up chairs so that a book cover would face the wall or a laptop screen could be hidden from people walking down an aisle.

What about your computer setup?

Where are the computers located? Can someone use a computer without another person seeing their screen? If it's possible for you to move furniture, try arranging desks so that the screens are not facing out toward public spaces.

Does your library have privacy screens available for users?

Dig around your library to see if privacy screens are available and where they are located. If you have some available, how would users access them? Create signage or come up with a creative solution that lets users know they're available.

Use the space here to map out potential changes you could make to your library's space.

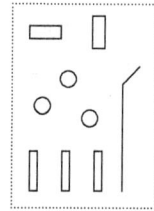

EXAMPLE

User Surveillance

How do you monitor users within your library? Many libraries have cameras to ensure the safety of both users and staff. While safety is always of the utmost importance, it can also lead to privacy violations. Cameras placed inside the library might be able to follow a user through the building, tracking their use and borrowing history. This footage could be viewed by library staff or requested by law enforcement. Everyone who enters a library should have the right to a private experience, free from an obtrusive eye in the sky.

Even if your library doesn't have cameras, you may still be violating the privacy of users by monitoring their behavior inside the building. Sometimes staff may have conscious or unconscious biases that lead them to follow certain types of people through a library space. Don't follow users around the library or peek at what is on their computer screens.

EXERCISE

Take a look at where your security cameras are pointing. Can they follow someone through the building and keep tabs on what they access? If possible, have security cameras only outside of the library.

Discussing Users

We all discuss library users with our fellow staff members. Sometimes it's necessary for security or for the academic enrichment of a user to share their name or other personal details with our colleagues. Many times staff just want to share an interesting interaction or express their frustrations after a long day. When discussing users, it's important to take a pause to decide if it's necessary to divulge who they are to another staff member.

Staff should never discuss one library user's behavior or library use with another user. If you live in a small town or serve a smaller library community, you might not even need to share someone's name for another person to figure out who you're talking about. Be vague with details that might expose someone without their consent. Also, always consider where you are before speaking. While it might seem at first glance that it is only you and a coworker at the circulation desk, another user may be within earshot.

EXERCISE

It can feel uncomfortable to stop a colleague when they're violating someone's privacy by sharing their personal information in a conversation.

Write up three ways that you might approach a coworker if you overhear them talking about a user.

1. _____

   _____

   _____

   _____

2. _____

   _____

   _____

   _____

3. _____

   _____

   _____

   _____

Overdue Items

Not returning an overdue book can be embarrassing for many users. For some, it means incurring punitive fines. These fines can prevent them from coming to the library or even graduating from college. While libraries will often delete the borrowing record of items returned, an overdue book may remain on your record for years. This is a ripe opportunity for a user's borrowing history to be shared without their consent.

Examples of Personally Identifiable Information (PII) include:

- Name
- Social Security number
- Birthdate
- Government issued ID number
- Financial account numbers
- Contact information (email, phone, address)

EXERCISE

Research how your library is notifying and discussing overdue materials with users.

K–12 Schools

If overdue book notices are printed and placed in homeroom teachers' boxes, fold and staple the notice so that only the student's name is visible. If students are notified in person, move to a private location to have the conversation so that no one can hear what material the student checked out.

Public Libraries

Does your library call users to inform them of overdue items? If so, develop procedures that require a user to verify their PII before staff disclose the title of the overdue item. No information should be given to anyone other than the cardholder. This includes minors.

Academic Libraries

How does your library handle requests from professors to recall items held by students? If necessary, develop a policy that allows the student's information to remain private. Professors and staff should not be given details as to who checked out the material.

Follow the Paper Trail

Libraries are palaces of paper. We hold vast quantities of information on the pages lining our shelves. We also hold vast quantities of users' PII in binders, desk drawers, and filing cabinets. A paper hunt in any library may turn up book requests spanning thirty years, volunteer forms from teens who now have teenagers of their own, library card applications, program sign-in logs, and pieces of scratch paper with user barcodes and search queries. Paper is still one of the most common ways that a user's privacy can be violated, and their information shared without their consent.

EXERCISE

Go on a paper scavenger hunt:

1. Collect any piece of paper you can find that has PII.

2. In the table below, write down the types of documents you find, where they are located, what PII they contain, if they are in a secured location, and the library's retention policies for them.

3. Then use the three subsections that follow the table to help you assess what to do with the documents you've found.

DOCUMENT TYPE	LOCATION	SECURED (Y/N)	PII	RETENTION POLICY

4. Now shred any document that has passed its life span, and secure any documents with user PII that you plan to keep.

Information Collected

A library should only collect the information needed for business operations. No information should be collected because you think it might be needed one day. This is especially true for PII. Review all the pieces of PII you are collecting from users. Ask yourself, "Why am I collecting this?" Then ask yourself, "Could I still perform my task without this piece of information?" If the answer is yes, then you don't need it. Take this opportunity to update your documents to collect the least amount of PII possible.

Library card applications often contain the most PII. Review what information you're collecting and determine what you can remove. Your library shouldn't need to collect identification numbers (de-tangle these from student IDs if at all possible), gender, Social Security numbers, or exact birth dates.

Storage

Where did you find the document? Was it sitting on a desk or in a drawer where a user could access it? Was it stored in a binder in the office space where a volunteer, student worker, or unauthorized staff member could take a quick peek? When people hand over their PII, they trust us to keep it safe. If you have documents that contain a user's PII, it needs to be secured in a place where only authorized staff can access it. Find a desk drawer or office where sensitive information can be stored. Where possible, store information in a space secured with a lock unless it needs to be accessed.

Retention

In your search, did you find documents that have outlived their usefulness? If your library does not already have a retention policy, now is a great time to create it. Your governing body may already have a policy that you can look to for guidance. It's rare that you will have a document containing a user's PII that needs to be kept in perpetuity. Everything has a life span, and it's important to regularly discard documents. Anything that contains users' PII must be shredded. Have a shredding party! If your library is unable to acquire shredders, there are services across the country that can shred for you.

Anonymizing Holds

Most states have laws in place that require public libraries to keep a user's library use private. Both the ALA's Code of Ethics and its Library Bill of Rights

insist that libraries respect and uphold a users' privacy in their use of the library. This means that we should not expose a user's reading, viewing, or listening habits to others. The number-one way that libraries violate this is through on-the-shelf holds. There are many libraries that use users' full names and library card numbers to identify holds. Sometimes, that library card number is a piece of sensitive data like a Social Security number. This is far from best practice because it allows users to see what others are reading and can also expose users' PII.

But what if you don't have any control over changing the holds slips? What else could you do to anonymize the process? Some libraries have opaque bags or paper slips that can go over books when they sit on the shelf.

Case Study

When you walk into a library in Aalborg, Denmark, you'll notice that the holds shelves are free of receipts. How do users find their holds without the classic receipt tucked into the books' pages? Staff use an app to scan the barcode on the item and then the barcode of the shelf where it will be placed. This generates an automated message that is sent to users with the specific location of their item. Using this system eliminates any possibility of violating a user's privacy, as there is no way of publicly displaying what items they have on hold.

EXERCISE

1. Go to your holds shelf and look at how the items are labeled. What did you find?

2. If your holds slip includes a full name and library card number, what could you use instead?

3. Talk with your circulation department about alternatives.

Current holds Information

_____

_____

_____

_____

Suggested changes

_____

_____

_____

_____

_____

Receipts

Even as we move further into the digital world, many users still love getting a physical receipt after checking out their materials. Parents hang them on the fridge to remember due dates. College students keep them tucked inside their course reserves. Sometimes the receipts get tossed into the trash, but often they are left behind inside a book for the next user to discover. Before computerized checkouts, it was common for someone to know who had checked out an item. All you had to do was look at the checkout card pasted on the inside cover. Integrated library systems (ILS) have made us rethink this approach, but many receipts still divulge a user's PII.

EXERCISE

Select a few items from your library and check them out. Use the self-checkout machines, and then try checking items out at the staff desk. Try different types of materials like a course reserve or a popular DVD.

Take a look at what information is on the receipt. What do you find?

- Do your receipts include any PII?

- What information would be necessary on a privacy-focused receipt?

If your receipt contains information that may expose a library user, try to get it changed. This might take a little technical knowledge or calling vendors to update the process. A sample receipt is shown on the right.

```
Esteemed University
Library
User name: Alex Parker
User ID: 35500648721
Title: Fahrenheit 451 /
Bradbury, Ray
Barcode: 67708992345671
Due: 10-31-22
Total items: 1
10/01/22 08:30
[www.esteemedu.edu]
```

Currently on your receipts	What you think should be on your receipts
_____	_____
_____	_____
_____	_____
_____	_____
_____	_____
_____	_____
_____	_____

Self-Service Discovery

QUICK TIP
School libraries that organize and label their materials by reading or grade level risk forcing students to disclose their reading capability to their peers. Use standard, viewpoint-neutral labeling in the library. **https://bit.ly/ LibraryLabel**

Your catalog is likely the primary way that users discover materials in the library, but it shouldn't be the only way. Many users may be hesitant to search for sensitive topics by using the online public access catalogs (OPACs) or by asking a library worker directly for the material. Users should be able to access all the materials in your library without asking for them directly or even by using one of your OPACs. If your library currently keeps titles behind the desk and only accessible by request, consider why and ask if this is necessary.

Work with the administration to develop policies that address privacy and uphold students' First Amendment rights. For more information, read the AASL's "Position Statement on Labeling Practices."

Teens: Help Yourself

If you're a teen looking for information on a sensitive topic, you can find the materials yourself if you know the call numbers they're cataloged under in the Dewey Decimal System. For example, you can look for the following call numbers on the shelves.

Abuse/Incest	362.76 and 362.78
Abusive Relationships	362.8292 and 362.88
Acne/Skin Care	616.53 and 646.726
Aids/HIV	616.9792
Alcohol	362.292
Anorexia	616.8526
Birth Control	363.9609 and 613.94
Body Changes/Puberty	612.661
Body Image	306.4613 and 616.852

For more privacy, use the self-checkout machines.

Source: www.ala.org/yalsa

EXERCISE

1. If appropriate for your type of library, create handouts on sensitive topics that can be discovered without users having to interact with the staff.

2. Walk through your library to determine all the ways a user can access the physical collection.

3. What barriers are there to access? If someone can only find an item through a digital search or by speaking to a librarian, what could you do to allow for self-service?

CHAPTER 4

Data Lifecycles

Libraries promote themselves to users as havens from data collection and analysis. However, user data is everywhere and with it comes a multitude of opportunities for it to be compromised. It is overwhelming to consider all the different types of systems, policies, and procedures relating to user data. This often prevents libraries from addressing data privacy risks. You can mitigate that overwhelming feeling by understanding the data lifecycles in your library. Understanding how user data travels through the library will empower you to create policies and procedures that put user privacy first.

In This Chapter

Data, Privacy, and the Library

User data collected by libraries can be divided into two types of personally identifiable information: data about a user, and data that is linked to a user.

PII 1: DATA ABOUT A USER

- Name
- Physical or e-mail address
- Date of birth
- User record number
- Library barcode
- Demographic information, including grade, year, major, and department

PII 2: DATA ABOUT A USER'S ACTIVITIES

- Search and circulation histories
- Computer/Wi-Fi sessions
- E-mail and chat transcript
- IP address; type of operating system or browser (digital fingerprint)
- E-resource access
- Program attendance

Each category contains data that can identify a real-world individual. You can
identify a person just by their activities; in fact, researchers have been able to
identify individuals from data sets that only contain their search queries.

The Library User Data Lifecycle

The library user data lifecycle helps to break down how user data is handled.
It can also tell you how you might be putting your users' privacy at risk. There
are six stages in the cycle: collection, storage, access, reporting, retention, and
deletion.

1. Collection

Collection is one of the most crucial stages in terms of protecting user privacy.
This stage is where you figure out what data is collected by an institution and
why it is collected. **Data that is not collected cannot be leaked or breached by
other parties.**

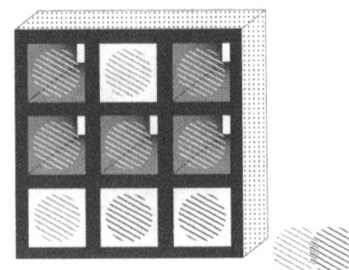

QUICK TIP
Turn off settings that
collect or store user
data that the library
does not need.

The Library User
Data Lifecycle

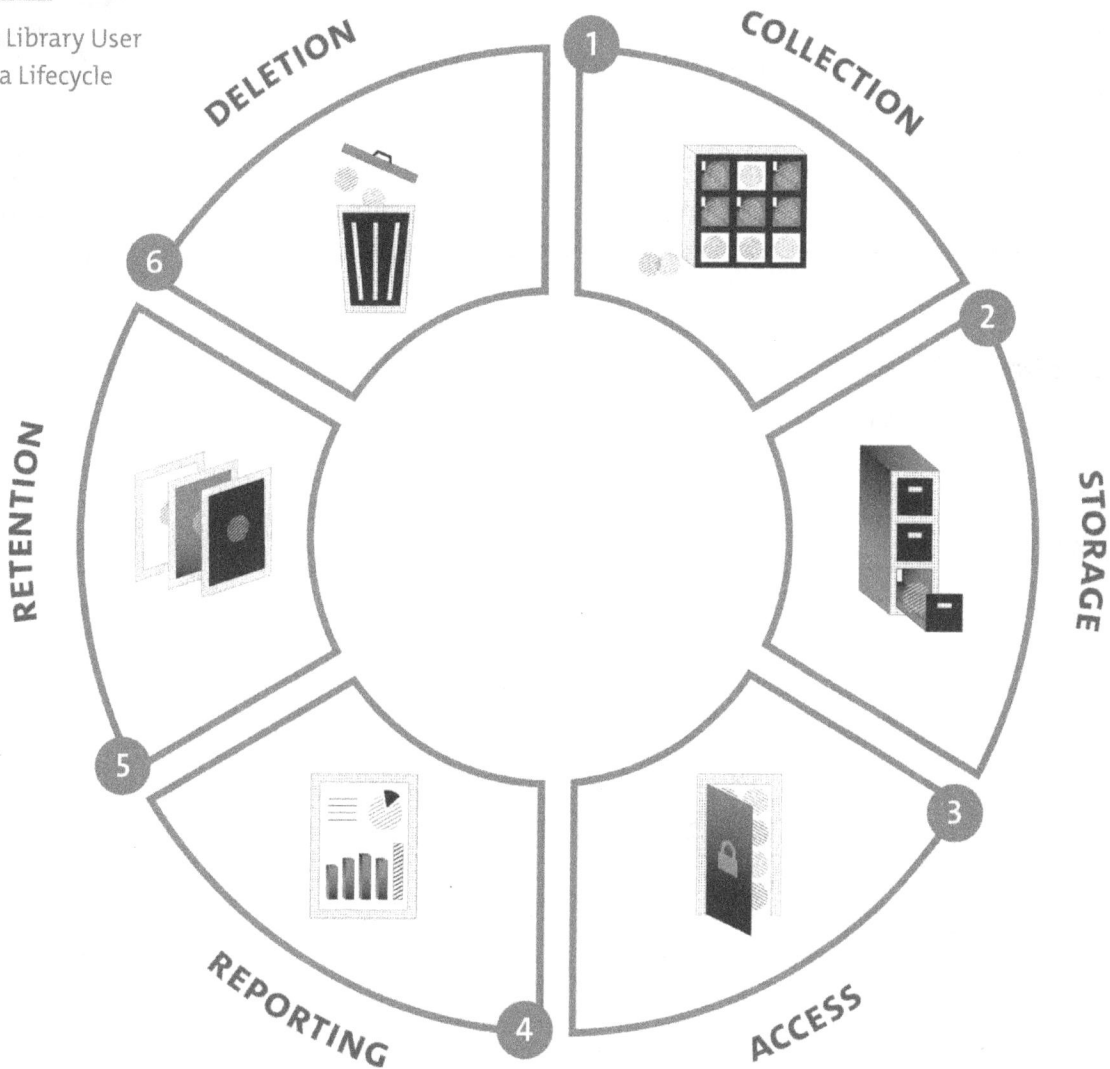

DELETION

6

COLLECTION

1

2

STORAGE

RETENTION

5

3

REPORTING

4

ACCESS

EXERCISE

What user data is collected at your library? The following list includes some common places user data is collected. Where else are you collecting user data at your library?

- Integrated library system
- Computer reservation system
- Library instruction data
- Data analytics software
- Your work e-mail account
- Reference or information desk chat logs

- _____
- _____
- _____
- _____
- _____
- _____

EXERCISE

Data FOMO (fear of missing out) is a thing! User data should only be collected if there is a specific operational need for it.

Review a user record to determine why data is being collected. Choose one piece of PII from the record and ask a coworker (or yourself) why it's being collected. After asking, "Why?" the first time, ask it again. Do this five times or until you can no longer answer why.

Data Point from User Record

- Why is this information collected?

_____

_____

Why? _____

Why? _____

Why? _____

Why? _____

_____

2. Storage

This stage covers the physical and electronic storage of user data at the library, in the cloud, or with a vendor. When thinking about where user data is stored, consider if multiple versions of the data are living in various places. The same data sets could be on backups, multiple desktops, e-mail, or even in a printout on someone's desk. Libraries should also consider what data sets that are stored in the same place could potentially be combined with each other to identify users. This is especially pertinent when raw (unmodified) user data from different systems is combined into one place, such as a data warehouse or a data analytics application.

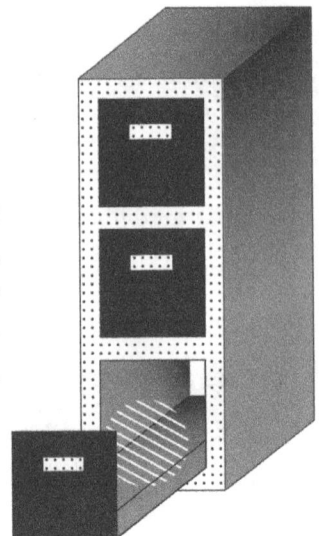

EXERCISE

Scavenger Hunt

User data should be stored in the least number of places possible. Having multiple copies spread out in various locations increases the risk that the data will be exposed or breached. Think of a type of user data collected at your library, and then go searching for all of the locations where it might be found. For each location, determine if the data is stored securely. A "secure location" might be a locked cabinet or a password-protected file.

- What user data did you find?
- Does this data need to be stored in multiple locations?

DATA LOCATION	SECURED (Y/N)	HOW IS IT SECURED? HOW WILL YOU SECURE IT?

For items containing user data that is not secured, consider the following:

- Store paper documents in locked desks or cabinets when not in use.
- Require individual user log-ins on all computers.
- Place electronic equipment in a space that has controlled entry (e.g., a locked room or storage area).
- Require log-ins for public-facing staff computers and mobile equipment, including multi-factor authentication, if possible.

3. Access

Physical access includes access to servers, computers, mobile devices, paper documents, and the spaces that contain any of those physical items. Electronic access includes user access levels in various systems and applications for both staff and vendors. Physical items that contain or have access to user data should be secured in locked areas and digital items that contain user data should only be accessible with a password. For digital files, practice the "principle of least privilege," providing staff members with access to the least amount of user data that is necessary to perform specific tasks.

EXERCISE

Perform a self-evaluation to determine if you have the appropriate level of access to a library application or system that handles user data. (See the table below.) Remember, everyone should be restricted to the lowest level of user data that is absolutely necessary for them to do their job. These different levels of access could apply to integrated library systems, vendor products, social media accounts, Google Drive folders, and so on.

If you are a supervisor or someone at your library with control over staff accounts, perform this same evaluation for all applications or systems to determine if each individual has the appropriate access levels.

APPLICATION OR SYSTEM	ACCESS LEVEL (CORRECT, SHOULD BE LOWER, SHOULD BE HIGHER)

Perform an annual audit of the access levels for staff for both electronic and physical access to user data. Use chapter 5, "Privacy Audits," for assistance in this process. Here are a few more things you can do:

- Deactivate the accounts of staff members who are no longer working at the library.

- Change user permissions for staff who have changed positions or gained/lost job responsibilities.

- Look at which vendors have user accounts and determine whether they still need access to the system.

4. Reporting

Reporting user data can take many forms, from internal dashboards for staff (such as checkouts and gate counts) to publishing library data as open data. Libraries should be cautious in how and what data they report, as this can be a way to inadvertently share users' PII.

What to Watch Out for

- Giving access to unmodified user data to all staff members
- Publishing raw user data in public sources
- Sharing user data with marketers and resellers, including the user data collected by vendors
- Being a "good citizen" while helping with law enforcement requests— by giving more information than requested under a warrant or sub- poena, or even giving information to law enforcement without one

How to Protect User Privacy

- Offer aggregated data through dashboards and canned reports.
- Create policies and procedures for the publishing of data to external audiences. This can include conducting privacy risk audits of data sets that are marked for publication.
- School and academic libraries should consult with legal counsel regard- ing the Family Educational Rights and Privacy Act's policies on educa- tional record disclosure.
- Does your library have a procedure for law enforcement requests? If not, or if the policy has not been updated for a while, here are a few resources from ALA (www.ala.org/advocacy/privacy/lawenforcement) to start the process:
  - » "Responding to Law Enforcement Inquiries: Suggested Guidelines"
  - » "Law Enforcement Inquiries: Key Concepts"

5. Retention

How long the library keeps user data depends on several factors, including legal regulations and operational considerations. Every library should have a retention policy. Your local governing body (school, city, county) may already have a retention policy that you can follow. There are very few items containing user data that should be kept forever. Make sure to check local and state regulations too. Some data may be exempt from retention regulations.

A library consortium should have retention policies and procedures for its member libraries to ensure the same level of user privacy throughout the consortium.

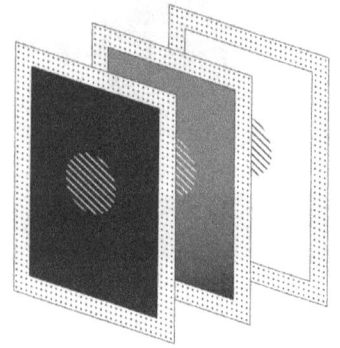

EXERCISE

Create a record retention schedule (like the one below) for library data, including user data, system backups, and logs. Ensure that the schedule is in compliance with local and state regulations.

DATA	FORMAT	WHAT DATA IS RECORDED?	WHERE IS IT LOCATED?	WHO HAS ACCESS?	HOW LONG IS THE DATA KEPT?
Library card application	Paper Electronic	Name Date of birth Address Email Telephone	Circulation desk ILS server	All staff with ILS access	Paper applications are shredded after one week. Digital applications are purged every 30 days.

6. Deletion

QUICK TIP

Hard drives or disks that are no longer in use should be destroyed. If there are plans to reuse a drive that contained user data, ask the IT department to help wipe it before use.

The deletion of data includes the disposal of records on electronic and physical media, as well as electronic files. Once a data point has been collected, it is very hard to delete it from existence. User data can even be exposed by not properly disposing of electronic equipment. (There have even been cases where sensitive information has been pulled from a discarded copy machine's hard drive.) Along with proper electronic equipment disposal, make shredding a regular part of your library's healthy privacy practices. Any paper that includes a user's PII (including e-mail) should be shredded.

EXERCISE

Have a shredding party. Schedule a time for staff to bring paper documents containing user data to shred at their location (staff should not travel with documents containing PII). If the library does not have access to a shredder, there are companies that will shred for a fee.

CHAPTER 5

Privacy Audits

Privacy is essential to the exercise of free speech, free thought, and free association. It is the responsibility of all libraries to ensure that their procedures and policies are designed with privacy in mind. If users lose their privacy, then they lose one of the things that makes a library so great: the freedom to seek information without fear of reprisal. Privacy audits enable libraries to explore how they handle user data, build a healthy privacy culture, and institute practices that align with the laws and ethics of the profession. This chapter provides step-by-step instructions for libraries of all shapes and sizes on how to perform their own privacy audits.

In This Chapter

What Is a Privacy Audit?

Privacy audits are procedures to ensure that your organization's goals and promises of privacy and confidentiality are supported by its practices, thereby protecting confidential information from abuse and the organization from liability and public relations problems.

A privacy audit provides a library with an opportunity to examine:

- How privacy matters are handled at all levels
- The flow and storage of data
- The role data plays within the organization
- Staff training about privacy matters
- Existing and needed privacy policies
- User privacy and confidentiality

This is an ongoing process, not a one-shot project. Audits will look different depending on the size of the library and the level of control that staff have over the library's technology infrastructure.

Why Are Privacy Audits Important?

In today's society, there is almost no place a person can go to seek out information without being tracked. Libraries have an ethical and democratic duty to be that place. When people are being watched, they change their behavior. A library that monitors and shares a user's information is no longer protecting intellectual freedom. Libraries should make every effort to provide a private place where people can exercise their rights to information access. Libraries can do this by performing regular privacy audits.

Every library needs to perform audits to understand how they and their vendors, partners, and administrators are handling user data. Even if your library is one room with one person on staff, you can ask a core set of audit questions. Understanding what your library's current practices are is the first step in crafting privacy-minded procedures and policies. With an increased reliance on third-party vendors, libraries are not able to have full control over users' data. However, a privacy audit will assist the library in being transparent with users about how their data is handled by the library and its vendors.

Building the Audit Framework

A privacy audit will cover a wide breadth of information, allowing you to dig deep into all areas of your library that interact with user data. The first step is to brainstorm all the places you will need to audit.

EXERCISE

What are the different places in your library that collect user data? Examples may include:

- Integrated library system
- Volunteer paperwork
- Social media
- Learning analytics software
- Website
- Student dashboards

Where is user data collected in your own library? List all the places here:

_____

_____

_____

_____

_____

_____

Core Questions

Once you've identified all the areas in the library that interact with user data, you'll want to ask yourself a set of "core questions." Keep these questions handy and ask them any time you, a partner, or a vendor is planning to collect user data. The questions will help you to collect the least amount of data needed and ensure that it's stored securely and is deleted according to a regular schedule.

EXERCISE

Pick one of the places in your library that collects user data. Answer the following core questions:

- What information do you collect?

_____

_____

- Why do you collect it? Do you need to collect it?

_____

_____

- How do you collect it?

_____

_____

- Who has access to it?

_____

_____

- What are the storage and retention policies/procedures?

_____

_____

_____

■ What are the current best practices and policies?

_____

_____

_____

_____

Is the user data shared with or collected by third-party vendors?

■ What vendors are used by your library?

_____

_____

■ What information is shared with or collected by the vendor?

_____

_____

■ Is the information collected by the vendor necessary for business operations?

_____

_____

■ What are the vendor's privacy policies, and do they align with those of the library?

_____

_____

What changes need to be made to ensure the privacy and security of user data?

_____

_____

Using Guidelines and Checklists

The core questions are a great starting place for any audit. The next step is to dig deeper and align your library with the privacy guidelines established by the American Library Association. ALA has created a set of guidelines and checklists that are available to help librarians, libraries, schools, and vendors to develop best practices for online privacy, data management, and security.

These guidelines and checklists were created for every library, of any size, to be able to use. The checklists are broken down into three priority levels:

- Priority 1 items are actions that all libraries can take to improve their privacy practices. These actions should be achievable by every library. They are the must-do items.

- Priority 2 items are actions that may be more difficult to implement, depending on the level of technical expertise (and other factors) in a library. However, these actions can usually be taken by larger systems and those with more control over their IT systems.

- Priority 3 items are actions that usually can only be taken by those libraries with a deeper technological understanding and resources. Some of these actions will be optional.

You can use the checklists (listed below) as part of the audit process. They will enable your library to be in alignment with the ALA guidelines and give you insight about current practices and policies.

EXERCISE

Read through all of the checklists that are available at **www.ala.org/advocacy/privacy/checklists**:

- Privacy Checklist Overview
- Vendors
- Data Exchange between Networked Devices & Services
- Public Access Computers & Networks
- Library Websites, OPACs, & Discovery Services
- Library Management Systems
- Students in K–12 Schools
- Assistive Technology

Then select the priority level your library would like to meet.

☐ Priority 1 ☐ Priority 2 ☐ Priority 3

EXERCISE

Complete ALA's "Privacy Checklist Overview" below. As you complete the checklist, ask yourself, "Is our library already doing this?" or "Is our library doing this, but it needs work?" Or, if you're not doing it at all, ask "What does our library need to do in order to complete this checklist item, and who's going to do it?"

PRIVACY CHECKLIST OVERVIEW	STATUS	STAFF ASSIGNED	DUE DATE	NOTES
Create a privacy policy that addresses the collection of user information. For guidance see the Privacy Policies Field Guide.	☐ NOT STARTED ☐ IN PROGRESS ☐ NEEDS WORK ☐ COMPLETED			
Destroy all paper records with user data that no longer have a business need, such as computer sign-in sheets. Keep any future records in a secure location.	☐ NOT STARTED ☐ IN PROGRESS ☐ NEEDS WORK ☐ COMPLETED			
Ensure all existing security certificates for HTTPS/SSL are valid and create a procedure for revalidating them annually.	☐ NOT STARTED ☐ IN PROGRESS ☐ NEEDS WORK ☐ COMPLETED			
Decide who in the library will handle requests for personally identifiable information of users from law enforcement officials and other third parties.	☐ NOT STARTED ☐ IN PROGRESS ☐ NEEDS WORK ☐ COMPLETED			
Ensure there is a formal process in place to address breaches of user data directly under library control or maintained by third parties. The library should notify affected users when they become aware of a breach.	☐ NOT STARTED ☐ IN PROGRESS ☐ NEEDS WORK ☐ COMPLETED			
Purge search history records regularly, ideally when the individual computer session ends.	☐ NOT STARTED ☐ IN PROGRESS ☐ NEEDS WORK ☐ COMPLETED			
Purge circulation and interlibrary loan records when they are no longer needed for library operations. Any user data that is kept for analysis should be anonymized or de-identified and have access restricted to authorized staff.	☐ NOT STARTED ☐ IN PROGRESS ☐ NEEDS WORK ☐ COMPLETED			
Complete the additional privacy checklists found on the ALA website.	☐ NOT STARTED ☐ IN PROGRESS ☐ NEEDS WORK ☐ COMPLETED			

Performing the Audit

If you are at a larger library, you will want to establish a team to complete the audit. Smaller libraries may find themselves with a team of one. That's okay. Even if you don't have the ability to make large sweeping changes, plan to audit whatever you can. Ask those core questions and identify the areas where you can make changes.

EXERCISE

1. **Create a spreadsheet for each of ALA's privacy checklists.** Only add the items from the priority level that your library is following. Also, create documents where you can answer the core questions for each of the areas of your library that handles user data.

2. **Assign tasks.** Establish who will be responsible for seeing if the library is currently in compliance with a checklist item. Will that same person be responsible for bringing the library into compliance? Identify who will research and document the answers to the core questions.

3. **Build a timeline.** Create due dates for completing checklist items and answering core questions. If changes need to be made, when do they need to be completed?

4. **Document your findings.** Everything you audit should have a document that outlines your findings. If you discovered changes that need to be made, determine who has the authority to make the changes. Bring your documentation to the appropriate staff to make a case for new policies and procedures.

You may have to interact with units outside of the library such as campus or school IT. Set up a meeting to discuss the audit. Do they already perform one regularly? Can the ALA checklist items be added to their audit process?

Telling the Audit Story

An audit doesn't just happen in someone's head as they think about all those core questions and checklist items. You must have a method for capturing your findings and noting what changes are going to be made and when. Each area of the library being audited should have a document detailing the findings. The documents will be a reflection on the checklist items, answers to the core questions, and any recommendations or future actions that need to be undertaken or are in the process of getting started.

Consider sharing your findings documents with stakeholders inside and outside the library. This provides transparency and highlights the importance of privacy in the library.

EXERCISE

How will your library tell its audit story? Detail methods of transparency and list any stakeholders that the audit should be shared with.

Rinse and Repeat

Your first privacy audit will be the most challenging one and will require the most work. Establish how often the library will perform audits and then stick to a schedule. Remember that after each audit, you should go back to your policies and procedures to ensure that they are up-to-date.

EXERCISE

Determine a schedule for a regular audit. What position at the library will take the lead? What resources will your library need to support this ongoing work?

CHAPTER 6

Privacy Policies

Policies define and shape the culture of a library. How a policy is written says a great deal about the library and gives users a pathway to understand how the library operates. Privacy policies, in particular, are notorious for being overly complicated and are written to obfuscate rather than educate. Libraries can break the traditional privacy policy mold by learning how to write a policy that is clear and easy to understand. This chapter will help you to navigate through all of the vendor privacy policies, allowing the library to make informed decisions before entering into contracts, as well as explain to its users how their data is being used by third parties.

In This Chapter

What Is a Privacy Policy?

Privacy policies tell library users what data is collected about them, their data rights, and how that data is used, shared, stored, and deleted. These policies also give users information about third parties that have access to their personal information, and direct users to vendors' privacy policies. Well-written privacy policies give users clarity on how the library and its vendors handle their personal information, and inform them about the laws that govern its use and disclosure.

So you're not the decision-maker or policy writer at your library? No worries! Use this chapter to ask questions about vendor privacy policies and to advocate for your library to write its own policy. Chapter 2, "How to Talk about Privacy," can help you have conversations with the stakeholders responsible for making changes.

Some school library workers may be unable to persuade decision-makers to create and have the school board approve a privacy policy. No problem. You can use this chapter to create an informal set of privacy guidelines and procedures that take into account state and federal laws as well as the Library Bill of Rights and Code of Ethics.

How to Read a Privacy Policy

Before we learn to write, we learn to read. The best writers are voracious readers, learning techniques and identifying pitfalls from the work of others. Privacy policies are notorious for being intentionally written to obfuscate (make unclear) rather than inform. They are written by lawyers to protect companies from litigation, not as a mechanism to aid in the understanding of the end user or to gain informed consent to use their information. By learning how to read privacy policies, you can start identifying when vendors have a privacy policy that aligns with your library's values and ethics. Reading the privacy policies published by corporations will also teach you how to provide clarity in your own policies.

In the subsections that follow you will learn about commonly used phrases and terms and policy red flags.

Understanding Commonly Used Phrases and Terms

"PERSONALLY IDENTIFIABLE INFORMATION" VS. "NON-PERSONAL INFORMATION"

- Personally identifiable information (PII) is information that can be used to identify a specific person. Some examples of PII include a person's name, Social Security number, birthdate, government-issued ID number, financial account numbers, or contact information (e-mail, phone number, address).

- Non-personal information will often include what operating system is being used, user analytics (what pages are visited or the time spent on a page), device ID, and IP address.

"INFORMATION YOU GIVE TO US" VS. "INFORMATION WE COLLECT"

- In order to use a service, including the library, we often have to give over at least one piece of personal information. When someone signs up for a library card, the information they give to us may include their name, address, and phone number. They are aware that this information was collected because they were part of the transaction.

- When an organization uses the phrase "information we collect," they are often talking about information that they gather without the user directly giving it to them. This may include a user's IP address, what operating system they're using, their borrowing history, the websites they've visited, their search history, and so on. Users are often unaware that this information is being collected, and its collection is usually a condition of use. In a privacy policy, this information most often falls under the category of "non-personal information."

A piece of data that might be considered non-personal information in one state or country could be considered personally identifiable information in another based on local laws. Also, multiple pieces of data considered non-PII may still be used to identify someone by analyzing them together.

"COOKIES"

Most privacy policies will talk about collecting cookies. These are small text files placed on a user's computer that collect personal data. This allows the website to recognize the user each time they return. Cookies can capture user settings, e-mail addresses, and other personalization settings. It's important to know the difference between various types of cookies so you can fully understand the privacy policy.

- Session or temporary cookies are only active while the user is browsing the site and are deleted when the browser is closed. For example, they may be used to retain items in a shopping cart.

- Permanent or persistent cookies remain active even after a browser has been closed. They may store a username, password, or personalization settings. Persistent cookies can also be used to track a user's interaction with the website.

- Third-party cookies are tracked by websites other than the one you're visiting and are most commonly used by advertisers and social media companies. They can track spending habits, online behavior, and demographics. If you've ever looked up something on one website and then seen advertisements for it on other sites you visit, it's because of third-party trackers.

Are you hungry for more cookies? The cookies listed in this chapter are just a few of the flavors available. To learn more about cookies, check out the guide from HTML.com, at https://html.com/resources/cookies-ultimate-guide.

"THIRD PARTY"

- This often-vague term is used in most privacy policies. Many companies want to share at least some user data externally with a third party. A third-party entity might be used for data analytics, customer relationship management, or even advertising. Because library use data is protected to some degree by laws in most states, it is important to ask vendors what information is shared and who the information is shared with, including third-party entities. You might understand and feel confident in the data security practices of your vendor, but do you have that same confidence in a third party?

"AFFILIATED BUSINESSES"

- Many businesses have direct financial ties to other businesses. Two companies are considered affiliated when one is a minority shareholder of another. Privacy policies may state that user data is shared with "affiliated businesses." This is not usually considered selling user data, even though your library users' information may be shared with an outside entity you did not contract with. Ask vendors to disclose what information is being shared and with whom.

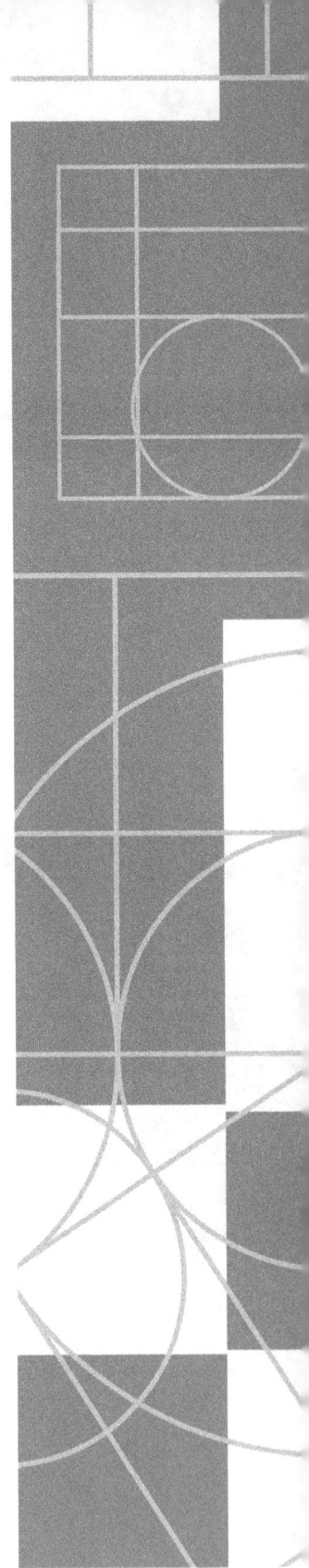

"COMBINE DATA" OR "DATA BROKER"

- Whenever we go online, data is collected about us. This data could be everything from our shopping habits to what sites we frequent, to which specific ads we've clicked on. Data brokers combine this data to create profiles of individual users. These profiles are sold to other companies, and this allows them to send targeted marketing to individuals. If a vendor uses trackers or certain cookies, it's important to find out if that information is being compiled and shared with data brokers.

"OPT-IN" OR "OPT-OUT"

- ALA's "Privacy: An Interpretation of the Library Bill of Rights" states that "users should have the choice to opt-in to any data collection that is not essential to library operations and the opportunity to opt-out again at any future time." Ideally, we want library users to have a choice when it comes to what data is collected and how it is used. If you see that a vendor's privacy policy has the default set to "opt-out," meaning the user has to manually choose to exclude themselves, ask the vendor if the policy can be changed to reflect the library's commitment to privacy by making the default "opt-in."

"CONSENT" OR "EXPLICIT/INFORMED CONSENT"

- Consent is a tricky concept online. Many websites say that they get a user's explicit or informed consent. However, that often just means ticking a box when registering for an account. A user is generally considered to have given their "regular" consent just by using the website. Most often, users have given their consent to a wide range of tracking just by opening up a website.

Red Flags

There are many commonly used phrases in vendors' privacy policies that should prompt you to question them about their practices. There are some things that you might not find as often in policies, but when you do see them they should immediately raise a red flag. When you find a red flag in a vendor's privacy policy, make a note and be sure to ask them to give you more details before entering into a contract with them.

SELLING/SHARING INFORMATION

Any vendor should be able to explain the lifecycle of a user's data. If you see a privacy policy that mentions sharing data with fourth parties, ask for specifics.

While you might trust the security and privacy practices of the vendor you're contracting with, do you know how this fourth party handles user data? Any mention of selling user data should be a huge red flag. Libraries already pay to access a vendor's platform; vendors should not also make money off of a user's data.

Example: *"Google uses the data collected to track and monitor the use of our Service. This data is shared with other Google services. Google may use the collected data to contextualise and personalise the ads of its own advertising network. You can opt-out of having made your activity on the Service available to Google Analytics by installing the Google Analytics opt-out browser add-on."*

STORING/TRACKING LOCATION DATA

Both libraries and vendors should always strive to collect the least amount of data required to offer a service. Using GPS coordinates to target the exact location of a user can mean that a person may be easily identified.

Example: *"When you access or use the Service, we may access, collect, monitor and/or remotely store 'location data,' which may include GPS coordinates (e.g., latitude and/or longitude) or similar information regarding the location of your device. Location data may convey to us information about how you browse and use the Service. Some features of the site, particularly location-based services, may not function properly if use or availability of location data is impaired or disabled."*

THIRD-PARTY INTEGRATIONS FOR USER AUTHENTICATION

Many people like the convenience of using their Facebook, Google, or Microsoft account to log in to various services across the Web. Sometimes these user authentication portals have embedded third-party trackers that give the platform access to a wide range of PII.

Example: *"We may receive information about you from third parties. For example, the Service may use Facebook or Google for user authentication. You should always review and, if necessary, adjust your privacy settings on third-party services before linking or connecting them to the Service."*

CLEAR GIFS, WEB BEACONS, AND TRACKING PIXELS

These are transparent images embedded on websites and in e-mails. They are mostly used in conjunction with cookies and track user behavior across the Web. They can also be used in e-mails to notify the sender when a recipient has opened a message. Web beacons cannot be denied or blocked like cookies. The most pervasive of them can even give overly specific location data.

Example: *"We use pixels to learn more about your interactions with email content or web content, such as whether you interacted with ads or posts. Pixels can also enable us and third parties to place cookies on your browser."*

E-MAIL COMMUNICATION (SIGNING PEOPLE UP FOR MARKETING E-MAILS)

The ideal setup for a user to access a vendor's product through the library would be one where they don't need to share their e-mail address to create an account. Their library card number and PIN should be sufficient. When this is unavoidable, it is important that the vendor use the e-mail address sparingly and not push advertising messages to the user.

Example: *"We will contact you through email, mobile phone, notices posted on our websites or apps, and other ways through our Services, including text messages and push notifications."*

DISCLOSURE OF INFORMATION

Vendors may get requests from law enforcement to disclose user data. This is part of the reason why we want vendors to collect the least amount of information possible. It is reasonable to see a notice in a privacy policy that states a user's information may be shared with law enforcement, but the vendor's ability to release users' information should be limited in scope. You can try to add contractual language that requires a vendor to notify the library when a request to disclose information is made, and to only release users' information when compelled to do so by law.

Example: *"Regardless of the choices you make regarding your information and to the extent permitted or required by applicable law, we may disclose information about you to third parties to: (i) enforce or apply this Privacy Policy or the Service Terms; (ii) comply with laws, subpoenas, warrants, court orders, legal processes or requests of government or law enforcement officials; (iii) protect our rights, reputation, safety or property, or that of our users or others; (iv) protect against legal liability; (v) establish or exercise our rights to defend against legal claims; or (vi) investigate, prevent or take action regarding known or suspected illegal activities; fraud; our rights, reputation, safety or property, or those of our users or others; violation of the Service Terms; or as otherwise required by law."*

OWNERSHIP OF DATA

The details around ownership of data can usually be found in the vendor contract. What you're looking for in a vendor's privacy policy is language that describes what happens to that data if a company is bought, sold, or transferred. A library should not be forced to share its user data with a new company until it has had the opportunity to enter into a new contract with them. Keep an eye out to see if the privacy policy clearly states if the library or its users have ownership over the data they provide directly to the vendor. Library user data should never be allowed to become a business asset of the vendor.

Example: *"In the event that a division, a product or all of Company is bought, sold or otherwise transferred, or is in the process of a potential transaction, personal information will likely be shared for evaluation purposes and included among the transferred business assets, subject to client contractual requirements and applicable law."*

SECURITY

While there are no 100-percent guarantees that user data can be secured, when a privacy policy uses soft language (e.g., "may," "try," "might," etc.) or calls out their inability to secure user data, it is a red flag. This language is used to absolve the company of legal responsibility should a data breach occur. Look for privacy policies that tell you how they secure the data, not that they are likely unable to do so.

Example: *"The security of your data is important to us, but remember that no method of transmission over the Internet or method of electronic storage is 100% secure. While we strive to use commercially acceptable means to protect your Personal Data, we cannot guarantee its absolute security."*

EXERCISE

Scavenger Hunt

Locate the privacy policy from at least one of your library vendors. Read through the policy and compare it with the lists of red flags and "commonly used phrases" in this chapter. Then answer the following questions:

- What vendor policy did you look at?

_____

- What red flags did you find?

_____

_____

_____

- What other red flags not listed (earlier) did you discover?

_____

_____

_____

- What else did you find that you didn't understand?

_____

_____

_____

- Take these red flags to your vendor (or library worker who is responsible for vendor products) and ask for clarity.

_____

_____

_____

How to Write a Privacy Policy

Writing in Plain Language

The Plain Writing Act became law in 2010, requiring federal agencies to use clear government communication that the public can easily understand. As we know from reading all those privacy policies, not many of them are written in plain language. By learning the principles of plain writing, you can craft a privacy policy for your library that your users will quickly understand.

EXERCISE

Visit the Plain Language website (www.plainlanguage.gov) and review all of the guidelines there. You will find information on how to:

- Write for your audience
- Organize the information
- Choose your words carefully
- Be concise
- Keep it conversational
- Design for reading
- Follow web standards
- Test your assumptions

PLAIN LANGUAGE TIPS

- Be conversational and use pronouns to speak directly to your reader: "We care about your privacy," not "The New Town Library cares about your privacy,"

- Add useful headings: "What information do we collect?"

- Be concise and descriptive.

- Avoid jargon and minimize abbreviations.

EXERCISE*

Understanding your audience is the first step in writing your policy. You need to understand who will be reading it so that you can write for them. A privacy policy written for third-grade students at an elementary school library will look different from one written for college students at a university. However, any policy should be written in plain language that delivers your message clearly.

Consider your privacy policy and answer the following questions:

■ Who is my audience?

_____

_____

_____

■ What does my audience need to know?

_____

_____

_____

_____

_____

_____

*The information and exercise found in this section come from www.plainlanguage.gov/guidelines/audience.

■ What's the best outcome for my library? What do I need to say to get this outcome?

_____

_____

_____

_____

■ What does my audience already know about library privacy?

_____

_____

_____

_____

■ What questions will my audience have?

_____

_____

_____

_____

■ What's the best outcome for our audience? What do I need to say to get this outcome?

_____

_____

_____

_____

_____

Writing Your Privacy Policy

There are several key areas to include in any privacy policy. There is no need to reinvent the wheel. The Library Freedom Institute has created a template for any library to use when crafting its policy, at https://libraryfreedom.org/resources. Review the template. What phrases or sections in it resonate with your own library's practices? What language can you use in your policy? All library policies should be reviewed and approved by your library's governing board and legal counsel before being implemented.

EXERCISE

Complete each section in this exercise to start drafting your privacy policy. Each of the questions in this exercise covers what should be a separate section of your policy. **If you complete all of these sections, you will have completed the first draft of your privacy policy!**

Privacy Statement—Your Right to Privacy

This is the section where you can tell users why privacy matters to libraries. Write details about your commitment to privacy values and ethics. Include links to applicable local, state, and federal laws.

Check out these library privacy policies for other wording suggestions:

- San José Public Library, Privacy Policy:
  www.sjpl.org/privacy-policy

- Multnomah County Library, Privacy and Confidentiality of Library Records:
  https://multcolib.org/privacy-and-confidentiality-library-records

- Privacy and Confidentiality in the Cornell University Library:
  www.library.cornell.edu/privacy

- Rutgers University Libraries, Privacy Policies:
  **www.libraries.rutgers.edu/about-rutgers-university-libraries/
  policies-and-guidelines/privacy-policy**

What Information Do We Collect?

Users have the right to know every type of information that is collected by the library. Include any and all PII and non-personal information you might collect. This section should also include information collected as part of any kind of analytics program. Including a link to third-party vendors' privacy policies is also helpful here. Be sure to include information that may be collected through e-mail, chat services, RFID, or any reference interactions.

This is a good section to include your retention policies. Let users know how long you keep any information, including their borrowing history. If you have a written retention policy, provide the link to it.

Who Has Access to My Information?

Remind users that their information is confidential, but also tell them who has access to it at your library. This is a good place to discuss policies that involve one user getting access to another user's information (e.g., a parent asking for their child's records).

How Do We Protect the Privacy of Students and Minors?

Many libraries serve users who may have specific privacy rights under local, state, or federal laws. If you serve students or minors, be sure to address how your library protects their privacy.

Our Website and Public Computers

This might feel like the most complicated section if you're unfamiliar with technology. If possible, seek out help from your IT department to fill out the details in each of the subsections below.

- **HTTPS**—Let users know what HTTPS is (it's a certificate that encrypts your network traffic) and that your library employs it on your website.

Does your library lack a secure website? Get a free SSL certificate with Let's Encrypt (https://letsencrypt.org).

- **Cookies**—Explain what cookies are (see the "commonly used terms" section in this chapter) and let users know what cookies your site uses. This subsection is likely to mostly involve teaching users about cookies.

- **Data and Network Security**—Let users know that you are actively working to prevent their data from getting into the wrong hands. You don't need to go into elaborate detail here, but avoid using phrases found in the red flag section like "we may protect your data" or "reasonable measures."

- **Public Computers and Connected Devices**—If your library offers Wi-Fi access, device checkout, or public computers, here is where you can tell users what protections are in place. Let users know how long you keep a log of their computer usage (hopefully not more than 24 hours) and what happens to their data when they log out of a computer or return a device.

Third-Party Vendors

Most library users think that anything they access from the library's website is part of the library. They are completely unaware of the vast third-party vendor network underlying much of the library's resources and collections. In this section, give a summary of the types of information that may be collected, used, and shared by these vendors. Provide a link to an easy-to-read and regularly updated page that has links to all of your third-party vendors' privacy policies. Also, include what the library's expectations are for vendors. This information may be found in the library's contracts or requests for purchase from vendors.

What Surveillance Is Used in the Library?

Many libraries employ some form of surveillance. Be upfront and honest with your users. Include details on security cameras and any body-worn cameras (including retention policies and who has access to the footage), facial recognition software, and smart speakers.

_____

_____

_____

_____

How Do We Handle Requests from Law Enforcement?

Detail the procedures in place when a request from law enforcement comes in to access a user's records. Include information about any training the staff has undergone to handle these requests.

_____

_____

_____

_____

Congratulations! You've just completed the first draft of your library privacy policy. Put your answers to all the questions (above) into one document and include the section headings too.

Your library may also want to include a "transparency report" as part of its privacy policy. Such a report would disclose statistics on the requests for user data or records made by government agencies over a certain period of time. These statistics might include the number of requests made, what agencies requested the information, and how many requests were fulfilled. Check out Google's "Transparency Report" for an example: https://transparencyreport .google.com.

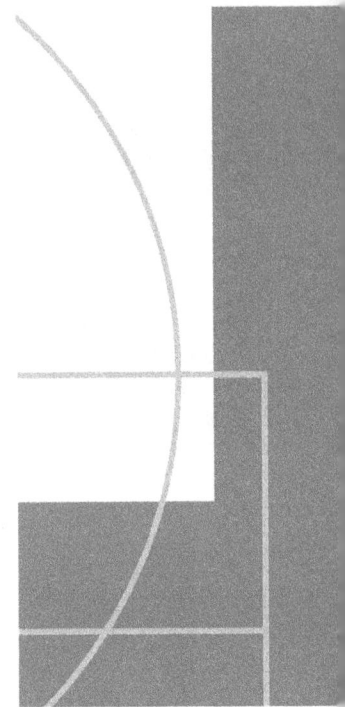

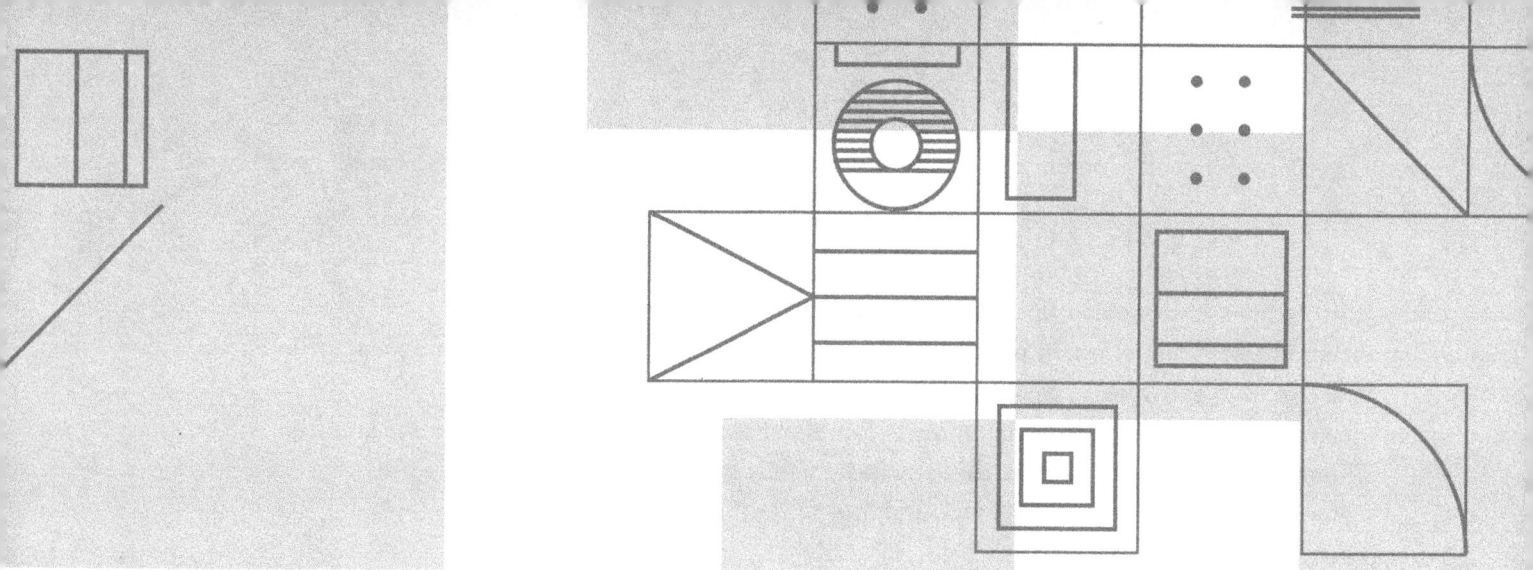

CHAPTER 7

Vendors and Privacy

Vendors help libraries serve users by providing critical infrastructure products and electronic resources. Libraries increasingly depend on vendors for these products and resources, but at what cost to user privacy? This chapter will introduce you to methods to protect users' privacy while evaluating and acquiring products and resources from vendors. The chapter will cover key strategies that libraries can employ to protect user privacy: contract language and negotiations, Requests for Proposal (RFPs), and vendor audits.

However, not all libraries have control over the vendor acquisition process. If the decision-making is out of your hands, this chapter can still help in identifying strategies to convince the decision-makers to keep user privacy in mind during the acquisition process.

In This Chapter

Who Controls the Decision to Buy?

Institutions have a wide range of purchasing processes. Some library workers have sole discretionary power over the acquisition of vendor electronic resources or software. In this case, you can choose your standards regarding privacy and refuse to purchase products that don't meet your standards. For library workers with full control over purchasing, this chapter can provide ideas of what to look for regarding privacy, and how to see if the vendor or the product meets those standards.

More commonly, no single library worker has complete control over purchasing. In some cases, library workers select some software and electronic resources, while other software is selected by a different part of the institution. In addition, the library may have control of the product selection, but the purchasing process may require the product being approved by another department, such as information technology (IT), legal, or the overall organizational administration or governing body. In that case, the vendor product may be held to those departments' privacy policies and standards, which might not be as extensive as the library's privacy policy.

EXERCISE

Investigate the vendor selection process at your library by listing your answers to the following questions in the table below.

1. Write the name of each library staff member involved in the vendor selection process.

2. What is their role in the selection process?

3. Do they consider privacy in evaluating resources?

4. Are there opportunities to discuss with them how privacy should be part of the evaluation?

STAFFER'S NAME	ROLE IN SELECTION PROCESS	IS PRIVACY A CONSIDERATION? YES/NO	CHANCE FOR DISCUSSION? YES/NO
Nancy	Approves invoices	No	Yes
Raul	Oversees RFP process	Yes	No

Don't know a person in the selection process? Are you wondering who you need to convince to become a library privacy ally? Check out chapter 2, "How to Talk about Privacy."

If you purchase or have access to vendor products through a consortium, ask the consortium what their privacy policy is and what standards they hold vendors to during the acquisition process.

Privacy Protections When Vendors Don't Align

The final decision to acquire vendor products may technically be made by the library; however, the political cost of not getting a particular database or product may simply be too high. When a product is very popular with users, or when a powerful person in your organization (professor, administrator, board member) pushes for a product, your library may need to acquire the product despite your concerns over user privacy.

Even when you can't control the selection of a product you feel doesn't protect user privacy, you can still take short-term actions to protect user privacy:

- Educate users through website notices before they leave the library website to navigate to a vendor resource.

- Use library instruction sessions and library e-resource product promotions as opportunities to educate users about the privacy risks of using vendor products and ways they can protect their personally identifiable information.

- Advocate for the adoption of aggregated metrics for internal use, particularly with software that identifies individual users.

- Do not retain personally identifiable information from vendor usage reports. Use aggregated totals when possible.

The What, When, and How of Evaluating Vendor Privacy

Selection—Shopping with Privacy in Mind

The first and best place to protect user privacy is during the vendor selection process. Libraries that have sole discretion as to which products to buy have the greatest amount of control in this area. For other libraries, this might not be the case. However, this does not mean that libraries can't have privacy-conscientious products! Selecting a vendor product can be overwhelming when there are a variety of choices, while at other times a dearth of choices can make the process extraordinarily underwhelming. In both cases, libraries still need to do their research into each vendor's privacy practices. The research done up-front can save you time down the road during the contracting process, as well as reduce the chance of surprises with regard to a vendor's privacy practices.

Having a systematic way to evaluate vendor choices can help save time and resources, as well as ensure that each vendor is evaluated with the same set of criteria. Depending on the organization and nature of the proposed purchase, libraries might be able to use a Request for Proposals (RFP) to collect information from vendors for evaluation. RFP templates can be updated to include questions about data privacy and security practices, as well as list privacy requirements that the vendor must meet in order to be considered for selection.

EXERCISE

Answer the following questions:

- How does your library's vendor selection process assess vendors' privacy practices?

- How can you incorporate privacy requirements and questions into that process, including in the RFP?

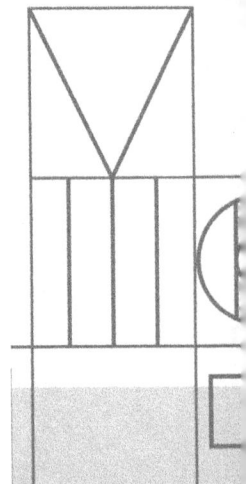

Evaluation Questions and Standards

Even if your library isn't required to go through the RFP process, you can use any of the following questions or standards to ask vendors while you're evaluating their products. To get you started, here's a short list of what to look for when researching vendors and their products for selection:

- Does the vendor have a publicly available privacy policy?

- What user data does the vendor collect, process, and disclose to third parties? What rights do users have to their own data? Is there an opt-out option?

- How does the vendor store user data? Is the storage encrypted? Where is the storage located? Is it hosted by a subcontractor? Is it stored outside of the country? Is it stored in the cloud or on a local server?

- Does the vendor meet specific information security standards, such as ISO/IEC 27001 or PCI-DSS, or use specific information security and privacy frameworks, such as the NIST Cybersecurity Framework and NIST Privacy Framework?

- What fourth parties or subcontractors does the vendor disclose user data to, and for what reasons?

- How does the vendor meet applicable federal and state legal regulations regarding data privacy and security?

Learn more about the following standards:

- **ISO/IEC 27001** is an internationally recognized and adopted information security standard that describes how to manage information security through information security management systems. Some organizations can become ISO/IEC 27001 certified after going through a rigorous certification process.

  www.iso.org/isoiec-27001-information-security.html

- **PCI-DSS** is an industry standard created by major payment card companies for securing payment card data.

  www.pcisecuritystandards.org/document_library

- **NIST CYBERSECURITY AND PRIVACY FRAMEWORKS** are guidelines and best practices for mitigating data security and privacy risks. Both guidelines are flexible enough to address specific organizational or business needs and risks around data privacy and security. These frameworks can be used separately or combined.

  www.nist.gov/cyberframework and www.nist.gov/privacy-framework

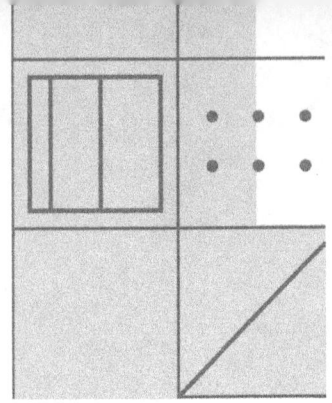

There are a couple of ways you can ask a vendor about their privacy practices:

- Tell them specifically what you want, such as "Vendor must use [specific level of] encryption for data storage and transit", or

- Ask how they meet a certain privacy criterion, such as "What are the security measures in place to protect user data in storage and in transit?"

Each way has its strengths and weaknesses. Asking if a vendor meets certain criteria can make evaluation quicker, but it might leave out important details about how the vendor meets those criteria. The details obtained by asking how a vendor meets certain criteria might be lacking and might require additional back-and-forth with the vendor.

EXERCISE

Think of a specific privacy criterion you want included in an RFP. When you approach the vendor, you can either:

- Tell them specifically what you want.

_____

_____

_____

- Ask how they meet the specific criterion.

_____

_____

_____

- Which of these would be the most effective way to ask the vendor, and why?

_____

_____

_____

Contracts and Licensing

QUICK TIP
The Vendor Contract and Privacy Rubric can assist you in evaluating the privacy provisions (or lack thereof) in contract language: https://publish.illinois.edu/licensingprivacy/contracts/.

Contracts and licenses are legally binding documents that state the expectations, rights, and responsibilities of all parties involved. They can also give vendors and other third parties rights to collect, process, and disclose user data, thereby raising the risk of compromising user privacy. With some advanced planning and careful reading, however, you can identify these privacy risks and negotiate with the vendor for more privacy-friendly terms.

Contracts' use of legal language can make them very dense and oblique for the average library worker reading them. Contracts might say that the vendor protects user privacy, but the vendor's privacy standards may not be the same as your library's privacy standards.

Contract negotiation can be a stressful and complicated process. Identifying areas you're willing to compromise on, as well the deal breakers, before the negotiation process begins can help. Do not be afraid to end negotiations over deal breakers! There are other vendors who might have better privacy practices. Additionally, a vendor might be pressured to change its contract or its practices if enough libraries refuse to sign or renew contracts with it because of deal breakers.

EXERCISE

Here are some examples of language from actual contracts. You can see the variety of approaches to privacy. What possible privacy risks or protections can you find in the examples?

1. "We take privacy very seriously. While we do log information on visits, queries, and other site activity, this information is for evaluating the effectiveness and usefulness of [product name] only. All specific visit information is treated confidentially and anonymously, and is never shared with any other party, including the participating distributors. Aggregated data is shared with distributors."

2. "The Parties agree to maintain the confidentiality of any data relating to usage of the Licensed Materials by the Licensee and its Authorised Users. Such data may be provided to third parties in aggregated form only and shall not include any information relating to the identity of individual Authorised Users."

3. "Any and all transfers of personal information will be in compliance with applicable laws and regulations, including, the Health Insurance Portability and Accountability Act ("HIPAA"), the Health Information Technology for Economic and Clinical Health Act ("HITECH"), the Family Educational Rights and Privacy Act ("FERPA"), and [State] Statutes §817.5681."

4. "Licensor shall be entitled to hold and process the personal data of Participating Institutions and Authorized users as defined in applicable privacy and data protection legislation; make such information available to (i) business partners, sub-contractors and/or suppliers who provide products, or services to Licensor; (ii) our branches; either of whom may be outside the European Economic Area for legal and administrative purposes in order to fulfil its obligations under this Agreement."

Answers

1. They admit that they track user behavior. Aggregated data is shared, but not PII. The statement "We take privacy seriously" has no legal meaning.

2. Aggregated data is shared, but no PII data is shared.

3. Anything not covered by HIPPA (not relevant), FERPA, HITECH, and local state laws is fair.

4. Personal data is shared with business partners, subcontractors, and suppliers in regions where the European Union's law on data protection and privacy (i.e., the GDPR) doesn't apply. The phrase "fulfil its obligations" is not defined, and could be broad.

Contract Red Flags

Here are some common red flags in contracts with vendors:

- The use of "reasonable" and other vague terms; these can signal an overall lack of transparency on data privacy and security

- Lack of definitions for key terms (such as "data")

- Indemnity/liability clauses that leave the vendor blameless when something goes wrong on their end

- Lack of information about what happens to library users' data after termination of the contract

- Lack of information about the vendor's responses to law enforcement or government data requests

- The vendor claims ownership over library user data

- The vendor reserves the right to resell or disclose user data to other third parties for marketing or other non-essential business purposes

- The vendor reserves the right to monitor users of its services or products (including the use of web analytics products or other tracking software or methods)

- The use of terms like "aggregated," "anonymized," or "de-identified" without defining these methods
- The vendor provides a URL to the privacy policy on the vendor's website; the policy on the website can change at any time without renegotiation of the signed contract

EXERCISE

Scavenger Hunt

If you have access to a vendor contract, read through the contract and compare it with the list of red flags given above.

1. What vendor contract(s) did you look at?

2. What red flags did you find?

3. What other red flags not listed (above) did you discover?

4. What else did you find that you didn't understand in the contract?

Take these red flags to your vendor or to the library worker who handles vendor contracts. Express your concerns and ask for clarification.

Making the Contracting Process Consistent

One way to make the contracting process more consistent across vendors is to include a contract addendum. Contract addendums (when reviewed and vetted by legal staff) provide standardized legal language about the level of privacy and security expected of the vendor by the library. Changing or amending the main contract language or including a contract addendum can address the common red flags listed earlier, as well as set responsibilities, rights, and expectations involving the following topics:

- Compliance with applicable federal, state, and local laws and regulations addressing data privacy

- Compliance with applicable industry standards and frameworks such as ISO, NIST, and PCI

- Legal jurisdiction of the contract; that is, what state or country's laws will apply when interpreting the contract or deciding a dispute

- Vendor privacy and security audits done by either an independent third party or self-administered by the vendor

- User rights to data, including access and deletion

- User rights to opt-out of non-essential data collection by the vendor, as well as the right to opt-out of the disclosure or selling of their data by the vendor to other third parties, at any time

- Abiding by the library's privacy and confidentiality policy when collecting, processing, and disclosing user data, and abiding by any laws or regulations applicable to library users' information

- Levels of access to and proper use of user data in the case of integrating with other library systems and applications

- User data retention periods

- Data breach and incident response

EXERCISE

Using the same vendor contract you just examined in the "Scavenger Hunt" red flag exercise, start a list that could lead to a contract addendum draft.

1. How can the contract be improved?

_____

_____

_____

2. What requirements around privacy do you expect/desire across all vendors?

_____

_____

_____

_____

Start drafting a contract addendum for your library. Work with your library's governing body and legal counsel to finalize the addendum.

Vendor Audits

Users trust the library to protect and secure their data, including when the library works with vendors or third parties to provide services and resources. How can libraries ensure that vendor data practices don't betray that trust? Libraries can ensure that vendors are following contractual terms and other legal obligations, as well as complying with specific data privacy and security standards and practices, by employing data privacy and security audits. These audits, conducted either by an independent third party or self-reported by the vendor, can identify any potential risks to user privacy, such as unnecessary data collection or disclosure; and potential weaknesses in security practices, such as how the vendor controls access to user data in its organization.

Here are a few examples of vendor audits:

- Santa Cruz Public Library's Vendor Security Assessment Questionnaire (VSAQ): www.santacruzpl.org/files/data_privacy/docs/SCPLVendor SecurityAssessmentQuestions.pdf
- Higher Education Community Vendor Assessment Toolkit (HECVAT): https://library.educause.edu/resources/2020/4/higher-education -community-vendor-assessment-toolkit

Keep the following in mind:

- APIs (application programming interfaces) and any LTI (learning tools interoperability) should be evaluated for privacy risk. If they integrate into course management software and individual students' accounts, then those vendors potentially have access to users' data.
- Apps that allow for access to vendor resources should also be evaluated for their privacy risk.

- Review vendor products for any additional "freebie" services or products not covered under existing contracts. For example, a vendor might provide access to another product at no cost in addition to the paid resources or services. A free product collects, stores, and shares data all the same as a paid product, but without any privacy protections provided in the paid product's contract.

Pushing for Privacy in Your Organization

If other units, such as the IT department or legal counsel, have a say in your acquisition process, learn their policies and standards around privacy. Those policies might cover only the legal minimum (legal compliance) of privacy protection, or they might only be concerned about privacy protections for the data that the library has to provide for the product. They might not be concerned about data the users can additionally provide, leaving that user data vulnerable to possibly harmful vendor data practices.

If you're part of a larger organization, find out if it has a privacy officer or someone with privacy in their job responsibilities. In academic institutions, these people may be focused on course management software or early warning student monitoring, and library databases and other resources might not be on their privacy radar.

EXERCISE

Pick a vendor product: an electronic resource, database, or system.

- What is the minimum amount of information a user must provide to use the basic version of this product?

_____

_____

- What additional information does a vendor require to use all the product features?

_____

_____

_____

Compare the two lists.

- How much additional user data is collected if the user decides to use the additional functions and services?

  _____

  _____

  _____

- Does the product encourage users to provide personally identifying data for personalized services?

  _____

  _____

  _____

  _____

INDEX

CPSIA information can be obtained
at www.ICGtesting.com
Printed in the USA
JSHW060216170523
41818JS00006B/27

9 780838 937303